Advance Acclaim for
If Your Adolescent Has Schizophrenia

"Truth rings out from every page of this incredible book that can be devoured in one sitting. It is exactly what parents need to know, delivered with precisely the right measure of science and personal story. Our son was diagnosed with schizophrenia six years ago at age 21. How I wish we could have had this book 12 years ago when the bewildering nightmare began. All my own strong opinions about the mental health 'system' are here. I found myself constantly exclaiming, 'Yes!'"

—Minnesota State Representative Mindy Greiling,
Chair of the National Board of Director's Policy Subcommittee on Children,
National Alliance on Mental Illness (NAMI)

"Unique and invaluable . . . concise, accurate, informative, and instructive. This is the first book I have seen that speaks directly and clearly to the primary questions and problems that overwhelm parents trying to cope with the tragedy of schizophrenia in their family. From making sense out of diagnostic uncertainty, to explaining about genes and the brain, to no-nonsense advice about treatment and rehabilitation, this book fills a gap that has long been needed."

—Daniel R. Weinberger, M.D.,
National Institute of Mental Health (NIMH)

"This book is a very informative addition to any parent's library. It tells caretakers what they need to know in a straightforward and practical manner. Schizophrenia is one of the most misunderstood and difficult mental illnesses for anyone to grapple with. Adolescents with new-onset schizophrenia need much support and guidance. This book gives parents the tools to help."

—Dr. Suzanne Vogel-Scibilia, National President,
National Alliance on Mental Illness (NAMI)

"The National Schizophrenia Foundation is always delighted to have new resources made available that will inform persons with schizophrenia and their family members about the disease and provide tools for dealing with it. First-person accounts are extremely important in allowing people to truly understand the reality of schizophrenia and the road to recovery. Kudos to Drs. Gur and Johnson!"

—Eric C. Hufnagel, President & CEO,
National Schizophrenia Foundation

"Whether this is your first venture into learning about the realm of adolescent schizophrenia, or your latest addition to a growing library, this book will be of invaluable assistance. With the perfect blend of scientific expertise and down to earth explanations, Drs. Gur and Johnson provide a very useful guide for all people affected by adolescents with schizophrenia and for their relatives."

—Ming T. Tsuang, M.D., Ph.D., D.Sc.,
Professor of Psychiatry, University of California at San Diego

"Parents must cope with illness in their child, and the challenge could hardly be greater than when the diagnosis is schizophrenia. This book provides expert knowledge, perspective, and guidance in a practical, reader-friendly format. The information will support each step in the recovery journey."

—William T. Carpenter Jr., M.D., Director,
Maryland Psychiatric Research Center

The Annenberg Foundation Trust at Sunnylands' Adolescent Mental Health Initiative

Patrick Jamieson, Ph.D., *series editor*

Other books in the series

*If Your Adolescent Has Depression
or Bipolar Disorder (2005)*
Dwight L. Evans, M.D., and Linda Wasmer Andrews

If Your Adolescent Has an Eating Disorder (2005)
B. Timothy Walsh, M.D., and V. L. Cameron

*If Your Adolescent Has an
Anxiety Disorder (2006)*
Edna B. Foa, Ph.D., and Linda Wasmer Andrews

If Your Adolescent Has Schizophrenia

An Essential Resource for Parents

Raquel E. Gur, M.D., Ph.D., and
Ann Braden Johnson, Ph.D.

The Annenberg Foundation Trust at Sunnylands'
Adolescent Mental Health Initiative

THE ANNENBERG
PUBLIC POLICY CENTER
OF THE UNIVERSITY OF PENNSYLVANIA

OXFORD
UNIVERSITY PRESS

2006

OXFORD
UNIVERSITY PRESS

Oxford University Press, Inc., publishes works that
further Oxford University's objective of excellence
in research, scholarship, and education.

The Annenberg Foundation Trust at Sunnylands
Annenberg Public Policy Center at the University of Pennsylvania
Oxford University Press

Oxford New York
Auckland   Cape Town   Dar es Salaam   Hong Kong   Karachi
Kuala Lumpur   Madrid   Melbourne   Mexico City   Nairobi
New Delhi   Shanghai   Taipei   Toronto

With offices in
Argentina   Austria   Brazil   Chile   Czech Republic   France   Greece
Guatemala   Hungary   Italy   Japan   Poland   Portugal   Singapore
South Korea   Switzerland   Thailand   Turkey   Ukraine   Vietnam

Copyright © 2006 by Oxford University Press, Inc.

Published by Oxford University Press, Inc.
198 Madison Avenue, New York, NY 10016
www.oup.com

Oxford is a registered trademark of Oxford University Press

Library of Congress Cataloging-in-Publication Data
Gur, Raquel E.
If your adolescent has schizophrenia : an essential resource for parents / Raquel E. Gur
and Ann Braden Johnson.
p. cm.
"The Annenberg Foundation Trust at Sunnylands, the Annenberg Public Policy Center at
the University of Pennsylvania."
Includes bibliographical references and index.
ISBN-13: 978-0-19-518211-8   ISBN-10: 0-19-518211-1 (cloth)
ISBN-13: 978-0-19-518212-5   ISBN-10: 0-19-518212-X (pbk)
1. Schizophrenia in children. 2. Schizophrenia in adolescence. 3. Children—Mental
health. I. Johnson, Ann Braden, 1945– II. Title.

RJ506.S3G68 2006   618.92'898—dc22   2005026317

9 8 7 6 5 4 3 2
Printed in the United States of America on acid-free paper

Contents

Foreword

The Adolescent Mental Health Initiative (AMHI) was created by The Annenberg Foundation Trust at Sunnylands to share with mental health professionals, parents, and adolescents the advances in treatment and prevention now available to adolescents with mental health disorders. The Initiative was made possible by the generosity and vision of Ambassadors Walter and Leonore Annenberg, and the project was administered through the Annenberg Public Policy Center of the University of Pennsylvania in partnership with Oxford University Press.

The Initiative began in 2003 with the convening, in Philadelphia and New York, of seven scholarly commissions made up of over 150 leading psychiatrists and psychologists from around the country. Chaired by Drs. Edna B. Foa, Dwight L. Evans, B. Timothy Walsh, Martin E. P. Seligman, Raquel E. Gur, Charles P. O'Brien, and Herbert Hendin, these commissions were tasked with assessing the state of scientific research on the prevalent mental disorders whose onset occurs predominantly between the ages of 10 and 22. Their collective findings now appear in a book for mental health professionals and policy makers titled *Treating and Preventing Adolescent Mental Health Disorders*

(2005). As the first product of the Initiative, that book also identified a research agenda that would best advance our ability to prevent and treat these disorders, among them anxiety disorders, depression and bipolar disorder, eating disorders, substance abuse, and schizophrenia.

The second prong of the Initiative's three-part effort is a series of books, including this one, that are designed primarily for parents of adolescents with a specific mental health disorder. Drawing their scientific information largely from the AMHI professional volume, these "parent books" present each relevant commission's findings in an accessible way and in a voice that we believe will be both familiar and reassuring to parents and families of an adolescent-in-need. In addition, this series, which will be followed by another targeted for adolescent readers themselves, combines medical science with the practical wisdom of parents who have faced these illnesses in their own children.

The third part of the Sunnylands Adolescent Mental Health Initiative consists of two websites. The first, www.CopeCare Deal.org, addresses teens. The second, www.oup.com/us/teenmentalhealth, provides updates to the medical community on matters discussed in *Treating and Preventing Adolescent Mental Health Disorders*, the AMHI professional book.

We hope that you find this volume, as one of the fruits of the Initiative, to be helpful and enlightening.

Patrick Jamieson, Ph.D.
Series Editor
Adolescent Risk Communication Institute
Annenberg Public Policy Center
University of Pennsylvania
Philadelphia, PA

If Your Adolescent Has Schizophrenia

Chapter One

Introduction: A Parent's Nightmare

My son . . . sees things that none of us see and I don't know how to
reach him.   —Anne Deveson, *Tell Me I'm Here:*
One Family's Experience of Schizophrenia

This is a book about schizophrenia, a serious mental disorder that usually appears in late adolescence or early adulthood, seemingly without warning. Schizophrenia is many things, not least a disease that affects all the people who know and love the person who has it. Since many people who develop schizophrenia are teenagers or young adults, the disease affects the parents of those children directly and painfully. Parents must watch as the child they know and love changes in ways they may not fully understand. At the same time, parents will most likely continue to be the chief caretakers of their affected children, often well into adulthood. For in the age of deinstitutionalization and managed health care, the family is the first line of defense against a serious, personality-altering, and potentially life-threatening chronic mental illness.

Schizophrenia develops gradually, over many years. Although in retrospect its emergence may seem obvious, for most parents the first episode of full-blown schizophrenia will probably come as a shock. As Anne Deveson, whose son Jonathan was diagnosed with the disease, recalls in her 1991 memoir *Tell Me I'm Here,*

> Had I been equipped with my present knowledge, it would have been clear that Jonathan had been heading for a breakdown for months, even years before it occurred. . . . But I was grappling with that age-old parental dilemma of balancing the danger of being over-reactive with making sure that I was not guilty of benign neglect. And then [his father] brought Jonathan into the kitchen and said, "I think he's sick." After that the days that followed were never quite the same.

This is a book for parents, teachers, guidance counselors, and anyone else who regularly comes in contact with kids in their late teens and early twenties, some of whom may well develop the symptoms of schizophrenia. The book is meant to be a practical and helpful guide to one of the most challenging conditions known to modern psychiatry, the day-to-day challenge of which falls most squarely on the families of the people who have it.

The scientific material presented here draws in part from the findings of a Commission on Schizophrenia, chaired by the lead author of this book, that was part of the Adolescent Mental Health Initiative spearheaded in 2003 by the Annenberg Foundation Trust at Sunnylands to address the increasing prevalence of severe mental illness (e.g., depression, anxiety disorders, eating disorders, and other conditions) among our nation's young people. The book draws from other sources as well and indeed could not have been written without the generous help of several parents who have been there, seen it all, and lived to tell the tale of raising a child with schizophrenia. They were uniformly delighted to have the opportunity to tell other parents what they themselves had to learn the hard way. Their names have been changed to protect their privacy, but the experiences they shared with us for this book are very real. We are grateful to them for their assistance, and to the extent this book is helpful to parents in a practical way, it is because we went to the source: parents of adolescents with schizophrenia.

A special thank you must go to a young man whom we are calling Paul, whose story can be found in Chapter 4. Paul is an unusually open and frank young man, who was eager to tell the story of his own mental illness for this book, so that it might help others. Ten years ago, Paul was in and out of psychiatric hospitals, in some doubt as to whether things would ever get better for him. Today, he is a paid advocate for young people who, like him, have spent or are spending the years of their late adolescence in hospitals rather than in school. Although he admits that he still struggles every day, Paul has so far risen to the challenges put in his way by his disease, and he is an articulate and forthright advocate on behalf of people with severe mental disorders.

Chapter Two

Understanding the Disorder:
What It Is and What to Expect

At first, Mike was just excited, but, as the night wore on, his manner became threatening, almost violent. My mother, father, and I were at a loss to handle the situation. Michael kept acting as if he would strike us. I could imagine the headlines: Son kills family and himself. I kept wondering how this could be happening to my family.

—James Wechsler, *In a Darkness*

Definition of Schizophrenia

Schizophrenia is a chronic and severe mental disorder that is characterized by a disintegration of the process of thinking, of emotional responsiveness, and of contact with reality. Early in the twentieth century, schizophrenia was known as *dementia praecox* (premature dementia), because of the disintegration or fragmenting of mental functions typically observed in people with the disorder. The term *schizophrenia* itself means "fragmented mind," referring to the schisms between thought, emotion, and behavior that characterize the disease. It is not the same as "split personality,"

> The term *schizophrenia* itself means "fragmented mind. . . ."

which is an altogether different illness now known as *dissociative identity disorder*. People with schizophrenia do not alternate between "good" and "bad" personalities.

Most people who develop schizophrenia have their first episode of illness in adolescence or early adulthood. It is very rare before age 11, and it is not usually diagnosed before age 18 (when it is called early onset schizophrenia) or after age 50. As a general rule, males will develop symptoms about three to four years earlier than females, with the peak ages of onset for the disease occurring between 15 and 25 for males and between 25 and 35 for females. In addition, over half of all males with schizophrenia are admitted to a psychiatric hospital before age 25, compared to only one-third of female patients. On the whole, females with the disease are more likely than males to have better social functioning and a better outcome with less negative symptoms and improved quality of life. Notwithstanding all the gender-related differences in how and when schizophrenia develops, it occurs equally across the sexes.

Some researchers have speculated on a theory of "season of birth effect," holding that people with schizophrenia are more likely to have been born in winter and early spring, and less likely to have been born in late spring or summer. Others have suggested just the opposite effect: In recent research conducted across six countries, a striking number of young people with a severe form of the disease were found to have been born in the summer months of June and July. Schizophrenia is distributed unevenly throughout the world—some geographic areas report more cases than others—and because of this, some researchers have hypothesized that the disease may have a viral cause. Other researchers, however, have speculated that schizophrenia is precipitated by social stress, based on the fact that it is more common in large cities than anywhere else.

Signs and Symptoms of Schizophrenia

Schizophrenia is a disorder of perception. What is "real" to other people is often not "real" to a person with schizophrenia, and vice versa. For example, the person may watch TV news and hear the news anchors talking about him, commenting on his behavior or his appearance, while a person without schizophrenia watching the same broadcast would hear the anchors talking about tax reform or a baseball game. The individual with schizophrenia has misperceived what he has heard or has misinterpreted what he has witnessed, assuming the content to have been focused on himself when in fact it was not.

One way to imagine what distorted perception is like is to think about a time in your own life when you "saw" something that wasn't there. Maybe it was dark, or perhaps it was dusk—you looked outside and thought you saw a person in the backyard, but soon realized it was really just your trash can. A trick of the half-light of evening or the full dark of night confused you and you misperceived the trash can: You thought it was a person but on closer examination you realized you had been wrong. Something like this happens to people with schizophrenia, with the crucial exception being that they do not realize on closer examination that they were wrong; they continue to "see" a person and to react accordingly.

Barbara, the mother of a son with schizophrenia who is currently doing well, remembers that he once described what it was like to her. "He told me that being psychotic is like dreaming, except you're not asleep. The important thing about the dream is, while it's happening, you have no awareness that it's not real. You're telling yourself this story and you don't think it's a story; you think it's really going on. And that's what it's like to be crazy." The movie *A Beautiful Mind*, about mathematician John Nash's struggles with the disease, provides an excellent means of experiencing this delusional thinking by presenting scenes as if they were "really" happening, as indeed they were to the character whose thoughts are being dramatized—it never occurs to Nash that his perceptions of events are anything but real. The movie, cleverly, takes his point of view of events surrounding him, which means that the audience sees things as he does, without realizing that much of what they are seeing is in fact delusional.

Positive Symptoms

The first episode of schizophrenia is usually defined as the first episode of psychosis, or break with reality, which is sometimes called a psychotic break. This episode generally marks the first time the person shows *positive symptoms* of schizophrenia, or symptoms produced by the disorder itself. The classic examples of positive symptoms of schizophrenia are *delusions* and *hallucinations*. Both types of symptoms can only be experienced subjectively, by the person who has them—they cannot be observed or shared directly. Because of this, we are dependent on reports from people who have experienced them for descriptions of what they are like.

DELUSIONS

A delusion is generally an irrational belief—for example, that one is all-powerful or persecuted or under the control of others—and is maintained by the believer in the face of overwhelming contradictory evidence. The ideas that make up delusions often seem wildly far-fetched to others yet are taken for granted by the people who hold them. Here is an example of a delusion, described

The ideas that make up delusions often seem wildly far-fetched to others yet are taken for granted by the people who hold them.

in Sylvia Nasar's 1998 biography of John Nash, also titled *A Beautiful Mind*:

> [In 1959, Nash] began to notice men in red neckties around the MIT campus. The men seemed to be signaling to him. "I got the impression that other people at MIT were wearing red neckties so I would notice them. . . ." At some point, Nash concluded that the men in red ties were part of a definite pattern [involving] a crypto-communist party.

Nash's belief that men in red ties were signaling him was part of his first psychotic episode, occurring early in the development of the disease. Because the red-tie delusion was an early manifestation of his schizophrenia, it was not a particularly well-developed or entrenched belief, and apparently was one he kept to himself. Not long after he had decided men in red ties were signaling him, though, Nash began to tell strikingly outlandish tales to his colleagues. In one dramatic example included in his biography, he began to speak to a colleague very loudly during someone else's lecture, asking:

> "Did you know that I'm on the cover of *Life* magazine?" Nash told [the colleague] that his photograph had been disguised to make it look as if it were Pope John XXIII. [The colleague] also had his picture on a *Life* cover and it too was disguised. How did he know that the photograph, apparently of the Pope, was really of himself? Two ways, Nash explained. First, because John wasn't the Pope's given name but a name that he had chosen. Second, because twenty-three was Nash's "favorite prime number."

This is a much more fully developed delusion, involving a prominent and important public figure, a popular magazine, and intricate reasoning to explain the belief itself. Nash was hospitalized about two months later, diagnosed with paranoid schizophrenia.

In another example of a delusion, this one potentially life-threatening, an 18-year-old boy told his father, Frank, that he had been commanded to "walk in the desert for 40 days and 40 nights, fasting until God's will had become clear to him." So determined was the boy to put this plan into action that he kept his plans to himself, pretending to take medication given to him in a psychiatric hospital until he was discharged, at which point he announced his intentions to his father. Although the father was able to intervene several times to prevent his son from roaming in the desert by having him hospitalized, this particular delusion was quite entrenched: even with medication, the idea of fasting in the desert for 40 days reappeared subsequently, usually at times of great personal stress.

HALLUCINATIONS

The other classic positive symptom of schizophrenia is the hallucination, or false perception of one or another of the five senses—sight, hearing, taste, touch, or smell. When hallucinating, a person experiences a sensory phenomenon as real even though it is not actually happening. Common auditory hallucinations include hearing a voice or voices commenting on one's actions, two voices arguing, or voices that speak one's thoughts out loud. It is possible, for instance, that the boy who was determined to walk in the desert heard God's voice telling him to do so. Sometimes people who have recovered are able to recall and describe their hallucinations, as in the case of Mark Vonnegut, who wrote of his successful struggle to recover from schizophrenia in his 1976 book, *The Eden Express*. In the following passage, Vonnegut reflects on the grandiose delusional thinking he engaged in at

> When hallucinating, a person experiences a sensory phenomenon as real even though it is not actually happening.

the time he was committed to a psychiatric hospital, which was punctuated with commentary from his auditory hallucinations, "the mysterious forces":

> Who was I that such powerful mysterious forces were buggering around with my life? One team would come through cramming my head full of new knowledge, the next would sneak in and erase all the new stuff plus a lot of the old. I'd be crucified and resurrected several times a day . . . it seemed like the voices were trying to help, trying to give me some clue about what was going on. As usual, it didn't help much.

Other types of hallucinations are described in the short story "The Yellow Wallpaper," written by feminist Charlotte Perkins Gilman in the 1890s and based on her own experience. In the story, a woman reveals her gradual mental breakdown through her peculiar obsession with and hatred of the wallpaper in the bedroom of a rented house in the country. Over time, she develops hallucinations involving the wallpaper:

> In the daytime it is tiresome and perplexing. . . . But there is something else about that paper—the smell! I noticed it the moment we came into the room . . . whether the windows are open or not, the smell is here. It creeps all over the house. I find it hovering in the dining-room, skulking in the parlor, hiding in the hall, lying in wait for me on the stairs. . . . The front pattern [of the wallpaper] *does* move—and no wonder! The woman behind shakes it! Sometimes I think there are a great many women behind, and sometimes only one, and she crawls around fast, and her crawling shakes it all over. . . . And she is all the time trying to climb through . . . I think that woman gets out in the daytime! And I'll tell you why—privately—I've seen her! I can see her out of every one of my windows!

What Gilman described are olfactory hallucinations—hallucinations involving smells—and visual hallucinations, involving sight. In 1887, the author herself spent some time in a sanitarium, where she received a "rest cure," which was state-of-the-art treatment for nervous breakdowns at the time. She later wrote that she almost lost her mind there, and would often "crawl into remote closets and under beds—to hide from the grinding pressure of that profound distress."

Negative Symptoms

Schizophrenia is also associated with negative symptoms, which are called that because they represent personality traits or characteristic behaviors that are *taken away* by the disease. The hallmark of the negative symptoms is a gradual withdrawal from the world, including from one's family and even from one's own self. Other common negative symptoms include loss of interest in things, poor grooming, and noticeable reductions in speech, emotion, and motivation. The speech reductions are of two sorts: *poverty of speech,* in which the person speaks little or not at all; and *poverty of content of speech,* in which the person does talk but conveys little meaning in what he or she says. The emotional reductions manifest themselves as the absence or blunting of the ability to express emotion verbally or physically. And the loss of motivation—or *avolition*—appears as the lack of will to act, as in the act of maintaining one's personal hygiene.

Negative symptoms are nowhere near as dramatic or as memorable as the positive ones, although they may be the ones to appear first. They are rarely described by the people who develop them, although the following passage is an exception to that rule—a vivid description of the negative aspects of schizophrenia by an 18-year-old English boy who had had the disorder for about a year.

> I am more and more losing contact with my environment and with myself. Instead of taking an interest in what goes on and caring about

what happens with my illness, I am all the time losing my emotional contact with everything including myself. What remains is only an abstract knowledge of what goes on around me and of the internal happenings in myself. . . . Even this illness which pierces to the centre of my whole life I can regard only objectively. But, on rare occasions, I am overwhelmed with the sudden realisation of the ghastly destruction that is caused by this creeping uncanny disease that I have fallen a victim to. . . . My despair sometimes floods over me. But after each such outburst I become more indifferent, I lose myself more in the disease, I sink into an almost oblivious existence. My fate when I reflect upon it is the most horrible one can conceive of. I cannot picture anything more frightful than for a well-endowed cultivated human being to live through his own gradual deterioration fully aware of it all the time. But that is what is happening to me.

In some ways, it is the negative symptoms of schizophrenia that are most difficult for other people to live with, and the most disruptive of daily family life. As the anonymous author of the above description makes clear, the hallmarks of the disease include the person's obliviousness, despair, and indifference to what is going on around him or her. Added to a characteristic lack of interest in personal hygiene and in keeping things tidy, these behaviors can be very trying for those closest to the person. In his memoir *Angelhead* (2000), author Greg Bottoms remembers the early days of his older brother's illness:

Michael's decline, both mentally and physically, was astonishingly fast. . . . His body softened dramatically, his hygiene could produce a gag reflex. Where he had once been inordinately handsome, he now had smears of blackheads across his nose, a double chin, greasy hair. All of this happened so rapidly that when I remember it I think I must be wrong, the physical deterioration must have taken two or three or even five years. But it didn't. It all happened in only several months. . . . We lived *around* him, not *with* him. He would go days without speaking to any of us.

Recognizing the Symptoms and What to Do About Them

One of the challenges of schizophrenia is its often subtle early development prior to the first psychotic break. Early symptoms of the disease—known as "prodromal" or preliminary symptoms that may begin two to six years before the first psychotic episode—may include

- Reduced concentration and attention
- Decreased motivation and energy
- Mood changes, such as depression and anxiety
- Sleep difficulties
- Social withdrawal
- Suspiciousness
- Irritability
- Neglected physical appearance
- Decline in academic performance and abandonment of previous interests

The problem with these symptoms is their vagueness: They can be easy to confuse, for example, with aspects of "normal" adolescence or with the effects of drug use. Moreover, not every one of these symptoms appears in every individual who develops schizophrenia, nor does every teenager who experiences some or even all of these signs go on to develop the disease.

Thus, for many parents, the first major inkling that their child is ill is the appearance of more overt signs of the disease, which may include

- Seeing things or hearing voices that are not seen or heard by others
- Exhibiting odd or eccentric behavior and/or speech
- Having unusual or bizarre thoughts

- Confusing TV or dreams with real life
- Communicating confused thinking that is hard to follow
- Behaving like a much younger child
- Showing severe anxiety and fearfulness

Some of the overt symptoms may be quite shocking and embarrassing. In her book *Mad House* (1997), one young woman, Clea Simon, remembers vividly the occasion on which it became totally clear that her brother Daniel, a brilliant 17-year-old who had just won early acceptance to Harvard, had lost his sense of appropriate behavior: He came out of his bedroom late at night, stark naked, and proudly exposed himself to his mother and his two younger sisters, smiling happily even as they screamed and yelled at him to go back into his room. Despite the inappropriateness of Daniel's behavior, particularly in front of his mother and sisters, it is easy to see how his family managed to overlook this very bizarre display at the time and fail to attribute it to potential mental illness, if only because it was more shocking than harmful. And some things are much clearer in retrospect. His sister points out that

> The very nature of serious mental illness lends itself to second-guessing. I've done this; I think most family members of the mentally ill do. Because we feel helpless to cure, we look to see if there was, instead, some triggering event we should have taken seriously. And we nearly always find something that we feel ought to have clued us in.

What parents can do is to take an active role in having a teenager they suspect of being disturbed evaluated by a qualified professional. This means that if your child's behavior seems especially unusual to you, you shouldn't ignore it—parents usually know their kids very well indeed and should trust their instincts. Different parents will respond to different signs of distress in their children. For example, Peter Wyden, author of *Conquering Schizophrenia* (1998), sought help for his son Jeff because of his persistent concerns that Jeff simply wasn't developing normally; the boy struck him as too shy, socially backward, and uninvolved in the world around him. For some parents, the signs of illness will be more obvious: Anne Deveson sought help for her son when he attacked her because he thought that rats were eating his brain. For others, the obvious signs will be all too familiar: Frank, the father of the boy who wanted to walk in the desert, recognized early that his son's delusions were symptomatic of schizophrenia because he had already experienced them in his own brother. For still others, the "obvious" signs could be subject to interpretation: Barbara, the mother of a boy who turned out to have schizophrenia, attributed his auditory hallucinations—in his case, hearing voices coming to him over the radio—to LSD use. But even if your adolescent has similar psychotic symptoms that he or she appears to get over, don't be lulled into thinking that everything is back to normal. It is *never* normal to have a psychotic episode; whatever its cause, professional assessment for it should always be sought. In short, *nothing is lost by checking out one's observations with an expert.* Even if the news is bad, you may feel relief once you get the diagnosis. Kate, whose son has schizophrenia, put it this way: "You know the enemy, and you have a name for it."

> *If your child's behavior seems especially unusual to you, you shouldn't ignore it—parents usually know their kids very well indeed and should trust their instincts.*

Advice From Parents to Parents Who Think Their Child Might Have Schizophrenia

Don't ignore

- Any hint or report that your teenager might hear voices
- Any story or anecdote your child tells you that has delusional content
- Any behavior or conversation that seems bizarre

Don't accept

- Teachers or doctors who tell you these signs are "just teenage behavior." If you think something is wrong, it probably is.

Be careful to

- Go along with whatever delusional or confused thing your child might say to you, especially if you're trying to get him or her to the hospital or the doctor. It's true to them and it won't help to get into a power struggle over what's real and what isn't.

Diagnosis of Schizophrenia: What Does It Tell You?

The diagnosis of schizophrenia should be made by a psychiatrist or other licensed mental health professional, based on a careful diagnostic interview that includes a detailed history. In the case of a teenager, this will be a particularly difficult diagnosis to make with certainty, because adolescence is famously a time of life in which instability and uncertainty are often present in the personalities of even the best-adjusted of kids. Diagnosis may be further confounded by the fact that many teenagers can meet established diagnostic criteria for schizophrenia as a result of substance abuse, conduct disorder, or attention defi-

Diagnosis in Psychiatry

Psychiatric diagnoses are based on the findings of research and observations made over time by doctors and others who work with mentally ill patients. They should not be viewed as final and authoritative definitions of well-established facts, but are more accurately understood as working rules that help clinicians who treat patients to classify them in a way that is useful and helps people to understand them. As the "Cautionary Statement" that introduces the American Psychiatric Association's 1994 edition of its *Diagnostic and Statistical Manual of Mental Disorders, 4th edition (DSM-IV)*, which is used by mental health professionals throughout the world, points out: "the specified diagnostic criteria for each mental disorder are offered as *guidelines* for making diagnoses." Psychiatric diagnoses are not written in stone, and ideas about them change all the time.

cit/hyperactivity disorder (ADHD)—or they may truly have all of these disorders at the same time.

Acknowledging these complications—the volatile nature of adolescence and the possible presence of coexisting conditions, also called *comorbidities*—many psychiatrists prefer to make the diagnosis of schizophrenia on the basis of information provided to them by one or both parents and possibly by the patient's friends. Patients themselves will be able to describe aspects of their experience as well, but because those with schizophrenia may find it difficult to report some or all of their symptoms and behavior accurately, it is extremely helpful to have information from the perspective of parents and friends to round out the picture. In addition, friends may be especially helpful, and perhaps more accurate even than parents, in reporting specific behaviors like substance use, a common activity among adolescents that can greatly complicate the diagnosis of any kind of mental illness.

A Disease With Many Faces

By definition, schizophrenia is a disturbance lasting at least six months and including a mixture of at least one month of two or more of the following symptoms:

- Delusions
- Hallucinations
- Disorganized speech
- Grossly disorganized or catatonic behavior
- Negative symptoms

See Appendix 1 for the whole of the *DSM-IV* diagnostic criteria for schizophrenia.

Moreover, the diagnosis of schizophrenia may involve a specific subtype, based on particular symptoms noted by the clinician making the diagnosis. Here are very brief summaries of three major subtypes and one disorder that is closely related to schizophrenia.

- *Paranoid schizophrenia*: Patients with this disorder are characteristically preoccupied with delusions and/or hallucinations that suggest they are being persecuted by others. Those with this subtype tend to develop it somewhat later in life than do those with other subtypes, and they are higher functioning. An example that received international attention is that of John Nash, a Nobel laureate, who had grandiose delusions, such as that he was on the cover of *Time,* disguised as the Pope. Another example is Jane, a college student with a part-time job who became suspicious that her coworkers were taking special notice of her. She thought that they exchanged glances when she entered the office and that during lunchtime they talked about her. She initially confronted them, and when they denied her allegations, she became more suspicious and isolated. She could no longer perform her duties, as she was more preoccupied with the "signals at work." She believed that her phone was tapped and that she was unsafe. When she sought professional help, she did so from a public phone, whispering so that those who "followed" her would not hear. She disconnected frequently and only after several calls was she persuaded that it was safe to be seen by a doctor.

- *Disorganized schizophrenia*: People with this type of schizophrenia (formerly called *hebephrenic schizophrenia)* tend to be bizarre and inappropriate in their behavior. They may choose to wear peculiar clothes, laugh inappropriately, grimace weirdly for no apparent reason, or talk about nonsensical ideas. One example is Josh, a young man in his late twenties who still lived at home with his parents. He had been ill for ten years, had never held a job, and had no friends. On visits to his doctor, he sat in the waiting area next to his mother, glancing around the room with a puzzled look and occasionally grimacing or bursting into laughter. He dressed sloppily, with shoes untied, and he invariably carried a bag full of papers. When he got to the doctor's office, he seemed remote and deep into his inner world, responding to the doctor's questions only intermittently. His thoughts were disorganized and difficult to follow, and the papers he brought out of his bag to show the doctor had nothing whatsoever to do with what he was saying. At the end of each visit, he had a hard time organizing his papers, and someone always had to help him put them back in the bag.

- *Catatonic schizophrenia*: This rare type of schizophrenia involves a disturbance of motor function: Patients may be in a stupor, mute, and physically rigid for hours, often in peculiar postures. Sometimes people with this type of schizophrenia will alternate between periods of stupor and wild agitation. Jeff, for example, was a young man in his late teens whose parents sought help for him because, according to them, "he stopped functioning," which turned out to mean that he lay immobile in bed with his eyes open, staring at the ceiling. During the examination, he was initially mute, answering none of the doctor's questions, but later in the interview, he repeated the last word of the examiner's questions over and over (echolalia). When the examiner moved Jeff's arms, they stayed in the same position until they were returned to his side. Because Jeff had stopped eating or drinking, he had to be hospitalized and ultimately required intensive care.

- *Schizoaffective disorder:* This disorder is not a subtype of schizophrenia but a related disorder, in which the disruptions of thought and perception of schizophrenia are combined with severe aberrations of mood. People with this disorder are likely to have delusions or hallucinations as well as mood swings that can include mania, depression, or both. Paul, whose story you will find in Chapter 4, has been diagnosed with schizoaffective disorder.

What Causes Schizophrenia?

In spite of over a century of research, scientists acknowledge that they know relatively little about the cause of schizophrenia. Among the many possible causes that have been explored, three areas in particular stand out as key targets of current research: brain abnormalities, genetics, and environmental factors.

Brain Abnormalities

Because certain abnormalities have been discovered in the brains of people with schizophrenia, compared to the brains of those without the disease, the most accepted hypothesis among today's researchers is that schizophrenia is a brain disease. For example, brain-imaging technology, including such methods as positron emission tomography (PET) scans, have identified reductions in metabolic activity in the frontal cortex of people who have been diagnosed with schizophrenia. These findings are most notable when the patient has performed a mental task during the scan, which is taken to suggest that the affected brain cannot react to what is going on around it in the world as efficiently as can a normal brain. In addition, neuropsychological studies of higher-level thought processes such as abstraction and concept formation indicate that people with schizophrenia, who perform poorly in both tasks, probably have reduced activity in the frontal cortex.

So far, researchers have not yet been able to formulate definitively just what it is that causes people with schizophrenia to have reduced frontal cortex activity, among other physical findings they have identified and associated with schizophrenia. Progress in finding the cause of brain dysfunction in schizophrenia has been slow, but this is explained by the extreme complexity of the illness. Many theories, however, involve the neurotransmitter systems of the brain.

How Neurotransmitters Work

The central nervous system is made up of thousands of cells called *neurons*, some of which collect information acquired through the senses of taste, touch, sight, smell, and hearing, which they send to other neurons for processing. To relay messages, the nervous system relies on neurotransmitters to carry information, in chemical form, across a tiny gap between neurons called a *synapse*. When a nerve impulse reaches a synapse, it causes the release of a chemical neurotransmitter, which diffuses across the gap and triggers an electrical impulse in the next neuron. The neurotransmitter does this by reaching a receptor site on the target neuron, a site designed to permit the neurotransmitter to bind to the host neuron. When a significant number of receptors are occupied, an electric impulse—a tiny electrical charge—is created and is sent across the host neuron. This is how the neurons in the brain and the rest of the nervous system communicate with each other, thereby regulating all functions of mind and body.

Diseases and injuries can disrupt the process by which neurons send messages to one another in various ways. The neuron where the message originates may produce too much neurotransmitter, or not enough, or the wrong kind; the host neuron may not have enough receptors, or too many; and receptors themselves can be the wrong shape, preventing neurotransmitters from binding to them. Many psychiatric disorders are known to involve inadequate quantities of a neurotransmitter in the brain—depression, for example, is treated by increasing the amount of serotonin in the brain—and many researchers have hoped to find such a link between schizophrenia and neurotransmitters.

THE DOPAMINE HYPOTHESIS

The neurotransmitter dopamine has long been studied for its role in schizophrenia, largely because some antipsychotic medications, such as chlorpromazine (Thorazine), seem to work by blocking dopamine receptors, thereby preventing dopamine from carrying messages across the relevant neurons. One version of the dopamine hypothesis assumes that the dopamine circuits in the brain are overloaded, causing people with schizophrenia to think they hear voices when they don't (hallucinations) and to act on false beliefs (delusions). Another version of the dopamine hypothesis suggests that while excessive dopamine activity causes these positive symptoms of schizophrenia, the negative symptoms are caused by the breakdown of dopamine into other chemicals over time. However, in one study only about two-thirds of schizophrenia patients have been found to have increased numbers of dopamine receptors, which suggests that dopamine overload is not the sole cause of the disease.

With the failure of the dopamine hypothesis to explain schizophrenia once and for all, research attention has turned to other neurotransmitters in the brain in the hope of finding additional explanations for the disease. Although so far, no definitive explanation has been forthcoming, researchers have found a number of anomalies among neurotransmitters in the brains of people with schizophrenia:

> *Researchers have found a number of anomalies among neurotransmitters in the brains of people with schizophrenia.*

- Tyrosine hydroxylase, a chemical related to dopamine, has been found in large quantities in the brains of people with schizophrenia, and researchers have speculated that an excess of tyrosine might create an excess of dopamine.
- Abnormally high levels of norepinephrine have been found in the brains of patients with schizophrenia.
- Because the antipsychotic drug clozapine (Clozaril) is able to treat the symptoms of schizophrenia by balancing the activity of both dopamine and serotonin, some researchers suspect that an excess of serotonin may be present in the brains of people with schizophrenia—unlike those with depression, who have inadequate amounts of serotonin.

Genetics

The question genetic researchers start with is: Does schizophrenia run in families? The question is answered by finding whether a close relative of a person with the disorder is at increased risk for developing it, compared with a similar individual chosen at random from the population at large. Since 1980, 11 major family studies have been reported in which the risk of schizophrenia was higher in first-degree (immediate family) relatives of schizophrenia patients than matched controls from the general population. On average, the studies determined that parents, siblings, and children of people with schizophrenia were twelve times more likely to develop the disease than the general population—5.9% risk versus 0.5%.

The goal of genetic studies of schizophrenia is to identify a genetic abnormality responsible for the disease. Once found, such an abnormal function would presumably shed sufficient light on what goes wrong in schizophrenia so that successful treatments could be developed and the abnormal function corrected at its source. So far, although a great deal of effort has gone into such studies, the results have been disappointing, most likely because there is no clear biological marker for schizophrenia. Because certain abnormalities of brain structure are present at the time of the first episode of disease, many researchers believe that schizophrenia is a neurological disorder beginning very early in life that for some reason does not lead to symptoms until late in childhood or early adulthood. Ideally, the next step would be to examine the developing nervous systems of people before they develop schizophrenia, but it is obviously very difficult to know in advance who should be studied.

The good news is that research goes on all the time, and some results are indeed promising. Some progress has been made

Genetic Counseling and Schizophrenia

With the increasing attention that the media is giving to genetics and particularly to the role of genetic factors in mental illness, people who are contemplating having children and who have a family history of schizophrenia may seek genetic counseling for issues related to the disease. Those who do typically ask three questions:

1. Is there a genetic test that can be performed to determine whether I have the gene for schizophrenia and so may pass it on to my children?

2. Is there a prenatal test to determine the risk that my unborn child will develop schizophrenia later in life?

3. What is the risk for schizophrenia to my children?

Unfortunately, the answer to the first two questions is no, there is not yet a test that can usefully predict risk for schizophrenia. The answer to the third question, however, is more reassuring. For the individual who has a parent or sibling with schizophrenia but who is him- or herself mentally healthy, the risk that his or her child (i.e., the grandchild or niece/nephew of the individual's relative with schizophrenia) will develop the illness is probably less than 2%.

in identifying genes associated with schizophrenia, which will in turn lead to opportunities to discover new targets for prevention and treatment of the disease. At the same time, researchers are investigating the role of genetic abnormalities in the brains of people with the disease, while others seek to understand how such genes influence perception, attention, and memory in schizophrenia.

Environment

If only because we know that not everyone at genetic risk for schizophrenia will develop the disease, it is assumed that environmental factors also play a role in its occurrence. For example, many observers assume that adverse environmental factors, such as maternal illness or trauma, that happen during fetal development will play a role in causing some cases of schizophrenia, while others have noted that poor socioeconomic conditions can affect the course of the disease in other cases.

Untangling the role of such factors in the development of schizophrenia will always be a challenge, if only because it is difficult to decide which is cause and which is effect. If a person with schizophrenia who is employed performs poorly because of hearing voices while on the job and gets fired, the result is almost certain to be an increase in symptoms of schizophrenia. Symptoms of the disease may have caused the person to get fired, but the effect of being fired can exacerbate those same symptoms. Suffice it to say that schizophrenia may be a biological disease, but the people who have the disease must live in the real world, which will have its own impact on their behavior. An example of this cause and effect relationship can be seen in the case of the 18-year-old boy who insisted he had to walk in the desert for 40 days and 40 nights: His father reports that even after the boy had been medicated, his "need" to walk in the desert tended to reemerge in times of great personal stress, as when someone close to him died.

> Schizophrenia may be a biological disease, but the people who have the disease must live in the real world, which will have its own impact on their behavior.

The presence of a number of specific environmental factors has been studied in people with schizophrenia. The role of stress in precipitating episodes of schizophrenia has been explored with mixed results, in part because of the difficulty in determining cause and effect—is the person's life stressful because he or she has schizophrenia, or does the person's illness arise because of stress? Other possible environmental factors that have

The "Schizophrenogenic Mother"

Most mental health professionals today agree that schizophrenia is in no way the parents' fault. However, some 50 years ago, when Freudian ideas about human behavior and psychology were more universally recognized than they are today, the development of schizophrenia was understood by many mental health professionals as a function of faulty family life. Ironically, this view of schizophrenia was not held by Freud himself, who called the disorder *paraphrenia*, a condition in which the only symptoms are delusions and hallucinations, and believed it to be unsuited to psychoanalytic treatment. One idea often discussed in the 1950s and 1960s was that of the "schizophrenogenic mother"—that is, the notion that a particular style of mothering could somehow induce schizophrenia in children. Such a mother was assumed to be cold and unmaternal toward her children, taking out her own personal unhappiness on them.

The idea that mothers could have schizophrenogenic relationships with their children was bolstered by the "double-bind" hypothesis of the origin of schizophrenia, which was based on the observation that some mothers regularly engaged in confusing and destructive communication that put their children in a no-win dilemma called a "double bind." A classic example of a double bind is this: A mother gives her daughter two identical sweaters for her birthday, a yellow one and a blue one. The daughter wears the yellow one first, whereupon the mother asks, "What's the matter; don't you like the blue one?" Obviously, the girl can hardly wear both sweaters first, and so this situation is one she cannot handle successfully. Observers of such communication dilemmas, many of them therapists who treated dysfunctional families, speculated that living in a family without ever being able to succeed in the simplest of communications without being caught in a double bind was enough to drive vulnerable children to retreat into fantasy to such an extent that they became "mad" or "crazy."

The idea that defective communication within families can render dysfunctional some children who are constitutionally at risk for psychological disorders has been reduced to the notion that psychiatry was deliberately "blaming" mothers for turning their children into individuals with schizophrenia. Probably some psychiatrists did "blame" parents, and probably some families do communicate in mutually destructive ways. But most mental health professionals today would agree that schizophrenia occurs whether parents create double binds or not.

been studied, albeit also with mixed results, include the previously mentioned "season of birth effect" and the role of city living in schizophrenia. Regarding the latter, the rate at which people develop schizophrenia is known to be consistently higher in cities, and cases are concentrated in the poorest areas of the city. But even though people have been studying this phenomenon since 1939, no one has yet been able to figure out which precise aspects of city life are responsible, in part because so many confounding factors are involved—cities are complex social settings, and the people who live in them must cope with multiple stressors all the time, any of which could challenge the coping mechanisms of those who are vulnerable to stress. Among the hypotheses that have been proposed to explain the situation is the possibility that social isolation within cities predisposes vulnerable individuals to develop the disease.

Schizophrenia and Related Problems

> [My brother] was famous in our new town of ten thousand white people as the good-looking bad boy. . . . He would take any drug, drink until he was facedown in some kid's suburban living room. But he still had one foot in reality at this point. His strangeness was attributed to the drugs my parents knew he did; he was an eccentric from a family tree full of eccentrics, a violent kid from a family in which violence, like alcoholism, ran in our blood, trickled down.
>
> —Greg Bottoms, *Angelhead*

Schizophrenia is a challenge for any family to handle all by itself, but virtually all families coping with a teenager who has schizophrenia will also find that they are called upon to cope with a raft of other problems. Because people with schizophrenia have experiences that are outside the reality shared by the people around them, it is common for them to disrupt classrooms, libraries, public parks, and their family homes. Because their behavior is often not what others expect, they sometimes get into trouble with the authorities, including teachers, parents, and police. Because they feel anxious or depressed a lot of the time, it is not at all un-

Virtually all families coping with a teenager who has schizophrenia will also find that they are called upon to cope with a raft of other problems.

common for them to turn to drugs and alcohol to help them feel better. And finally, because they are often extremely unhappy, many attempt suicide, and sadly some do in fact end their own lives. Parents of children and adolescents with schizophrenia will almost certainly be called upon to deal with one or more of these issues.

Problems in School

Those with schizophrenia tend to act according to the reality they perceive, rather than according to accepted social norms, partly because they experience a reality that is often at odds with everyone else's. They will sometimes seem very detached, distant, and preoccupied—going so far as to sit rigidly, without moving or speaking for long periods of time. At other times, they may move around restlessly, maintaining constant vigilance, always on the alert for unknown enemies likely to attack them. Obviously such behavior will not be particularly welcome in a school setting.

Perhaps even more disruptive of learning is the disordered thinking that is characteristic of schizophrenia. People with the disease are frequently unable to think straight and find it impossible to concentrate for any length of time. Their thoughts may come and go rapidly, with the result that to others they appear to be easily distracted and unable to pay attention to what is going on around them. They may also not be able to sort out the relevant from the irrelevant. Instead of concentrating on what is going on in French class, for example, a student with schizophrenia may be preoccupied with extraneous speculations about the presence of aliens in the classroom. Consider the following conversation, drawn from the biography *A Beautiful Mind*, between John Nash and his colleague, George Mackey:

> "How could you," began Mackey, "how could you, a mathematician, a man devoted to reason and logical proof . . . how could you believe that extraterrestrials are sending you messages? How could you believe that you are being recruited by aliens from outer space to save the world?" Nash looked up at last and fixed Mackey with an unblinking stare as cool and dispassionate as that of any bird or snake. "Because," Nash said slowly in his soft, reasonable, Southern drawl, as if talking to himself, "the ideas I had about supernatural beings came to me the same way that my mathematical ideas did. So I took them seriously."

Disordered thinking is a hallmark of schizophrenia. The person may be unable to organize his or her thoughts into logical sequences, with the result that they become fragmented and what we think of as "crazy." But as Nash pointed out, his ideas about alien beings made perfect sense to him, because they came to his mind the way all his other thoughts had.

Teenagers who develop schizophrenia are bound to find it difficult to function in the school setting. As the illness takes hold, they are likely to become less and less able to take part in regular classroom activities. Because their difficulties in school may well emerge long before the disease is diagnosed, parents may face experiences like the one described by Anne Deveson in her memoir about her son Jonathan, *Tell Me I'm Here*:

His childhood up to the age of twelve had been reasonably uneventful. . . . His written work was chaotic (nowadays he would probably have been assessed as dyslexic) but in primary school he got away with it, because he was so advanced in his general knowledge. . . . At high school, he began a dizzy spiral downwards. His writing became even more chaotic. He had problems concentrating and problems ordering his ideas. He seemed to find the environment of a big institution difficult to cope with. He found it hard to get up in the morning and was almost always running late. He became increasingly vague. He began to lose his friends, and he said that people were against him. . . . He said that school was stupid, the work was stupid, and he was stupid. He sat in front of his books with his head in his hands and you could tell that what was on the page wasn't reaching whatever was going on inside his head. He came home and paced up and down the kitchen, angrily telling me that people were scheming against him. Nobody liked him, he said. It was a familiar story.

In fact, many early signs of schizophrenia that emerge in school are not recognized for what they are. Jonathan, for example, wrote a paper for school that clearly indicated the presence of psychotic symptoms: He described himself as hearing voices and "walking along looking at himself walking along." He also described time as "stretching," while "spaces moved." The two school psychologists consulted by his parents at the time decided that he was fine, except for "communication problems" caused by his parents. Nor was theirs an unusual experience—Barbara remembers that even though her high-school age son openly acknowledged that voices spoke to him via the radio, no one at his school would even listen to her concerns about him.

In fact, many early signs of schizophrenia that emerge in school are not recognized for what they are.

Parents may have to intervene with their local schools to ensure that their child's academic needs are being met. For instance, younger children and adolescents with schizophrenia may need adjustments to the standard classroom, including smaller classes and the presence of teachers with experience in teaching students with psychiatric disorders. The reduced concentration and attention characteristic of schizophrenia may also require some modification of academic requirements, since some courses may be too challenging for some individuals to handle well. Information about obtaining appropriate accommodations in school for students with schizophrenia is provided in Chapter 4.

Problems With Other People

Every parent knows that two key tasks of childhood and adolescence are making friends and doing reasonably well in school, both academically and behaviorally. In adolescence, making friends becomes even more important, because a major task of that period of life is the gradual development of a self that can function independently of one's parents. Most teenagers accomplish this crucial task by shifting their allegiance from family to peers, which is why they dress alike, use the same slang, and consult each other on every purchase. These rituals of teen life are beyond the reach of kids who have or are developing schizophrenia, whose ability to interact normally with their peers is limited. In fact, the abandonment of preexisting relationships with siblings and friends may be one of the most valid warning signs of trouble to come. Other problems that may emerge include marked difficulty making friends and/or keeping them, and difficulty with any or all interpersonal interactions.

Most parents report the change in their children's behavior as much clearer in retrospect than it was at the time it was happening. As Peter Wyden writes in his book *Conquering Schizophrenia,* he realized after the fact that the "tremors of change" in his son Jeff's personality had been "easy to dismiss as normal expressions of puberty and postpuberty turmoil in an adolescent boy." Jeff's parents visited him in college and were thrilled to find him being "the proverbial life of the party . . . plotting gags with friends, too busy to pay much heed to us. . . . It was to be his last—and very temporary—outbreak of sociability." Looking back, Peter realized that for at least three years prior to that happy outbreak of sociability, Jeff had been introverted, uncommunicative, and extremely shy, especially with girls. Understandably, the whole family had expected him to grow out of it.

Eventually, though, Jeff abandoned the traditional life of the teenager, retreating more and more into what he called "moofing," which was defined by his father as "simply sitting about, looking lost, doing nothing . . . pushing was required to set him in motion." Looking back 30 years later, the father realized that Jeff's "moofing" was clearly of a piece with the onset of schizophrenia, an early harbinger of the negative symptoms of the disease. Here is a description of Jeff's behavior prior to his first psychotic episode, written at the time by his father:

> When [Jeff] buckles down to a job—writing a letter, reading a book— he is painstaking and very, very slow. I wonder whether this is part of his inhibitions or something else. In his preliminary SAT tests he performed way, way below the standards of his school grades because he finished so relatively few of the questions. . . . Jeff is, as always, *uninvolved.* This is perhaps the word that characterizes him best. He doesn't want to give of himself. Above all, he is "hasslephobic" and will do almost anything to avoid noise and trouble. It is as if he would like to trust things and people, and occasionally does, but is always fearful of being suddenly burned.

By the time Jeff had been hospitalized and diagnosed with schizophrenia, he had become a different person and someone whose behavior guaranteed he would be most unlikely to get along with anyone. As Peter writes, "My loving, bright, amusing son was not just very ill, but he had also turned distant, cold, bitter, insultingly rude, and had acquired other distasteful qualities. It would have been easy to dislike him intensely and give him hell all the time." More than a quarter century later, "it remains, at times, still a problem: How do you keep on loving a son who can be an unpleasant stranger?"

Problems With Siblings

The impairments that are part and parcel of schizophrenia will ultimately affect all relationships—parents, teachers, friends— but perhaps none will be so deeply hurt and frightened by a teenager's illness as his or her siblings. How hard it must be to watch, uncomprehending, while your beloved brother retreats into angry isolation in his room, or your admired sister turns mean and scary, for no apparent reason. And how hard it must be to watch your parents struggle to cope with the problems of living with a seriously troubled child. In her book *Mad House*, Clea Simon wrote of her experiences in a crumbling family that included not one but two teenagers with schizophrenia, her older brother and sister:

> Although our family fabric was fast unraveling, nobody talked to me about it. My parents were not sure what was happening, I think, and they sought to shelter me from their worst fears, seeing me as innocent of trouble at the age of seven or eight. I had my turtles and my stuffed animals. But I was also beginning to get the nightmares, the ones of total catastrophe, that would stay with me for years. . . .
> Daniel continued to dissolve, as if the brother I'd known were a torn cloth fraying at the edges; he seemed to shrink and change, become ragged and haphazard. Several times he left us—another attempt to

return to school, another hospitalization—and each time he returned diminished from the brother I knew. . . . At first, when he was doing well, he could still rally some of his former charm, his jaunty, teasing charisma. This served to render the inevitable declines that much harder to bear.

Not long after her brother left for good, her older sister Katherine became menacing where previously she had been merely annoying. Following a terrifying incident in which Katherine tormented her little sister's hamster to death, the writer learned to avoid being alone with her. "If I heard her coming toward my room, I would duck into my closet hiding place or sink deeper into the beanbag chair partly obscured by the door, in the hope that she would pass without a confrontation. . . . I became expert at holding perfectly still when she came to my door, unable to relax until she gave up calling to me and walked on."

The impact of the deterioration of first her brother and then her sister proved extremely stressful. "The shock of change, my apparent abandonment by my brother, and my betrayal by my sister happened too fast to be absorbed, and I was thrown into coping with floridly psychotic behavior. My brother was gone. My sister had turned into a monster, capable of violence." Her chosen response was to withdraw: "Life and death depended on escaping notice, and I chose to become as invisible as I could." Perhaps most difficult of all, she felt unable to turn to her parents. When she wanted to ask about her siblings' illness, "I saw in my father's eyes an overwhelming fatigue that silenced me with fear. What I saw in my mother's face, whenever I started to speak on the subject of Katherine's scary 'disturbed' episodes or Daniel's absence, was worse: I saw her grief for the child she felt she had already lost and grief for the child she was losing [to the illness]."

Whether one is the parent or the sibling of a person with schizophrenia, the net effect is the same: An important relationship has changed, by forces that are surprising with each psychotic episode that may occur. As Jay Neugeboren writes in his memoir *Imagining Robert* (1997), he witnessed such episodes in his brother over the course of many years, yet

> Each time it happened it did still take me by surprise, and each time it happened, it seemed unutterably sad and heartbreaking. How could it be that somebody who was so warm and loving, so charming, happy, and seemingly normal one moment—one day, one hour—could become so angry, wild, and lost moments later? And how could it be that each time it happened—no matter the years gone by—it felt as if it were happening for the first time?

Substance Abuse

It is highly likely that a person with schizophrenia is currently using or has used alcohol or street drugs, most commonly marijuana and cocaine. Although researchers all agree that people with schizophrenia and other mental illnesses are at risk of using drugs or alcohol or both, those who have studied the relationship between substance abuse and schizophrenia have measured it in different ways. For instance, one substance abuse expert stated in 2003 that 25% to 60% of individuals with mental illnesses are also substance abusers, noting that at the same time, as many as six out of every ten people who abuse drugs and alcohol also suffer from mental illnesses. A study published in 2004 looked at rates of substance abuse in 262 young people who were experiencing their first episodes of schizophrenia, and discovered that 37% of the sample could be diagnosed with a substance use disorder, that the substance abusers were more likely to be male, and that their response to treatment with antipsychotic medications was affected by their substance abuse. Finally, the National Mental Health Association believes that someone suffering from schizophrenia is at a 10.1% higher-than-average risk of being an alcoholic or drug abuser. It may be that all estimates of substance abuse are even higher among teenagers with schizophrenia, many of whom would probably be using drugs or alcohol even if they weren't sick, for much the same reason that a great many of their healthy peers use them: to feel good.

Indeed, the use of drugs and alcohol may serve as a sort of self-medication, with some individuals with schizophrenia finding that such substances decrease their anxiety, hopelessness, and depression and help them cope with the side effects of medications (discussed in the next chapter), while increasing their energy and motivation. Their abuse of such substances can also initiate them into the "fraternity" of the drug culture, where they may gain a social acceptance that may be increasingly absent from their peers; in other words, substance abuse can provide a means to a social network that helps people with schizophrenia to cope with the isolation and loneliness that their illness can cause.

Regrettably, though, studies have shown that drugs and alcohol also increase the potential for auditory hallucinations and paranoid delusion. Several street drugs, for example, can produce symptoms similar to those associated with schizophrenia, including speed, acid (LSD), and PCP (phencyclidine), all of which can produce hallucinations and delusions, as can prolonged marijuana use. In *Tell Me I'm Here*, Anne Deveson recalls a conversation she had with her son Jonathan about his drug use, which included marijuana and morphine-based cough syrup:

> One day he wandered into the house, with his lips pursed, and said, "Ever taken heroin? I just did and I saw God the Father and God the Son and God the Holy Ghost. And all these rings came in concentric circles, and I felt exultant. And I thought I heard from God, so I packed everything into a backpack, and went into the desert. I only lasted two days. I got my nervous breakdown. My revelation was that I was being a stupid idiot. . . . Junkies are cool; schizos are rejects."

An additional problem with the hallucinatory and delusional effects of some substances in a person with schizophrenia is their potential to mask the presence of the disease in the first place, causing the person to be misdiagnosed as merely high on drugs. Moreover, substance abuse by patients with schizophrenia can lead to all the usual problems found in people who use drugs and alcohol—impaired social and family relations, job loss, homelessness, debt, medical problems, run-ins with the law. Among adolescents with the illness, drug or alcohol abuse can also facilitate their social withdrawal from all but one or a few substance-abusing friends. As a teenager later diagnosed with schizophrenia, for example, Greg Bottoms's brother Michael abandoned all his former friends but one, with whom he shared amphetamines ("speed") while practicing karate every afternoon.

Cigarettes and Coffee

Multiple surveys have found that somewhere between 75% and 90% of people with schizophrenia smoke cigarettes, compared to about 50% of people with other psychiatric disorders and 30% of people in general. Cigarettes are the fundamental unit of currency in psychiatric facilities and a major focus of social interaction among patients, who prefer unfiltered, high-tar brands.

The reason for this striking affinity for cigarettes has been the subject of much research. Nicotine is known to reduce anxiety associated with the illness, reduce sedation resulting from medications, while also improving concentration in some people. It is therefore a desirable form of self-medication for some patients with schizophrenia. Surprisingly, people with schizophrenia have a lower rate of developing lung cancer than do people in general, even though they smoke so much. In all other ways, smoking is just as bad for the physical health of people with schizophrenia as it is for anyone else.

The observable affinity for caffeine is just as striking as that for smoking. Some patients with schizophrenia have been found to consume 30 or more cups of coffee per day (80 milligrams of caffeine each), in addition to multiple cans of cola (35 milligrams of caffeine each); moreover, some patients have been observed eating instant coffee direct from the jar. Greg Bottoms remembered that Michael drank huge amounts of a particular brand of instant coffee, mixed up in a giant thermos, day and night, in addition to smoking three packs of unfiltered cigarettes per day.

High intake of caffeine can of course produce nervousness, restlessness, insomnia, excitement, facial flushing, rapid heart beat, and twitching muscles, which anyone who has had too much coffee will know is not a particularly pleasant experience. It is therefore unclear just why people with schizophrenia consume so much caffeine, or what they get out of it. What is completely clear is that smoking and drinking coffee are two of life's greatest preoccupations for them.

The Risk of Suicide

"Suicide is a very real danger," writes now-recovered Mark Vonnegut in *The Eden Express* about his own repeated attempts to take his life during his struggle with schizophrenia, because "it may sometimes seem like a rational choice." An estimated 30% of people with the illness try to kill themselves, and an estimated 10% of them do in fact die by suicide. While it is much more common for adolescents to talk about hurting themselves ("I wish I were dead") or to threaten to do so ("If I don't get an A on my chemistry test, I'm throwing myself out the window") than it is to complete the act of suicide, as the parent of a child who suffers from schizophrenia, it's important to take all suicidal signs seriously. Kids who attempt suicide and kids who commit suicide share similar characteristics, and of those who do kill themselves, 40% have made at least one previous attempt.

The profile of the adolescent who commits suicide is often one of high achievement and perfectionist character traits, with suicide their desperate response to an event they consider a humiliating failure, like low scores on the SAT. In general, adolescents who are disturbed or vulnerable may also attempt suicide in response to life events, such as conflicts and arguments with friends or family, deciding that life is not worth living under such circumstances. At especially high risk for suicide are those individuals with schizophrenia who are highly educated, perhaps because they may realize the significance of their disease more clearly than other groups. Among other suicide risk factors, depression is high on the list, although individuals in the early phases of the illness (such as during the first psychotic episode) may attempt suicide as a result of hallucinations, paranoia, disorganization, or other symptoms considered more primary to psychosis.

Unfortunately, studies have repeatedly found that parents are quite often unaware of suicidal thinking in their adolescent children. You can help your child by being alert to potential suicidal triggers. Known risk factors that have been associated with suicide attempts made by adolescents include the following:

You can help your child by being alert to potential suicidal triggers.

- Mental disorders, such as major depressive disorder, manic episodes, or psychotic episodes
- Mood disorders in combination with substance abuse and a history of aggressive behavior
- Violent, aggressive, impulsive behavior
- Feelings of hopelessness and loneliness, combined with poor problem-solving skills and a history of aggressive behavior
- Depression alone, in girls more than in boys
- Loss of a parent prior to age 13
- Family history of suicidal behavior
- Exposure to family violence
- Availability of lethal methods, such as firearms, which are used in two-thirds of all suicides in boys and half of girls' suicides

In Chapter 3 (see p. 88), you will read about the best ways to handle potentially suicidal behavior in your child.

The Dangers of Doing Nothing

Faced with the possibility that your son or daughter has a mental disorder as serious as schizophrenia, with all its potential risks, you may feel overwhelmed or without a clue about what to do. Your initial reactions may be fear, disbelief, denial, grief, or perhaps even guilt that you're somehow responsible for his or her condition. Whatever you're feeling, it is extremely important that you not let your own thoughts and feelings paralyze you into inaction. Nor should you attempt to brush off concerns and dismiss your child's behavior as just a passing oddity of adolescence. Confronted with the visible signs that your child is in trouble, you'll need to take charge, face the problem head on, and act in your child's best interests by seeking professional help immediately. Such intervention can treat active symptoms of the disease and, if initiated early enough, can help stem the deterioration that the disease can bring.

It is important to be so proactive because the price of inaction can be devastating. The natural course of schizophrenia—that is, the way it develops without therapeutic intervention—begins with the first psychotic episode, usually the emergence of such symptoms as delusions or hallucinations. Most people will recover from their first episode, but that does not mean the disorder has gone away. Left to its own devices, the illness will develop into a chronic series of relapses into psychosis, followed each time by incomplete recovery, a process that eventually leads to persistent symptoms of disturbed perception and thought. Each subsequent relapse will be followed by less of a recovery than before, with a gradual but definite deterioration in the individual's function. Most of the progressive deterioration associated with chronic schizophrenia will take place within the first five to ten years after the first episode, which is why early intervention is so essential.

Without ongoing intervention, positive symptoms like hallucinations or delusions may fluctuate over time, but negative symptoms are likely to become more severe. People with schizophrenia never lose their vulnerability to stress, are perpetually at risk for relapse, and many face frequent hospitalizations. Poverty and homelessness are potential risks, especially for those who live in cities.

Future Prospects

Clearly, schizophrenia is a very serious disease, and most people who have it will not get better by themselves. Some do have only one psychotic episode and never have another, but most will experience repeated hospitalizations and episodes of renewed symptoms throughout their lives. Schizophrenia is not, in short, a condition that anyone ever "grows out of." Kate, a school psychologist and the parent of a son with schizophrenia, notes that it is not something that "a kid can just snap out of, so don't even try the 'tough love' approach—they can't help it, and they cannot get better all alone."

With early and ongoing intervention, however, many people with schizophrenia are able to live functional lives and to improve significantly. Prognosis in the first five to ten years after onset of the illness is affected by many factors, with the most positive outcome associated with the following:

With early and ongoing intervention, however, many people with schizophrenia are able to live functional lives and to improve significantly.

- A good support system of family and friends
- Late onset of the illness
- Sudden (rather than gradual) onset of the illness, with obvious precipitating factors
- Good social and vocational history prior to becoming sick
- Presence of mood disorder symptoms
- Presence of positive symptoms
- Family history of mood disorders
- High IQ

- High socioeconomic status
- Awareness of being mentally ill

Most important, an individual's prognosis is also influenced by the treatment that he or she receives. Although there is no cure for the disease, progress has been made in treating some aspects of the illness resulting in improvement and recovery of functioning. Such improvement might not be evident until the individual has undergone three to five years of treatment, with continuous gains noted over two to three decades. But the bottom line is that many people can be helped to live a productive life with the illness as long as they are involved in ongoing treatment programs, such as those discussed in the next chapter.

Chapter Three

Getting the Right Treatment for Your Child: Medications, Therapy, and More

Schizophrenia is so awful from so many different directions all at once, it's hard to know where to start. The important thing to keep in mind is that others have gone through it and come out in good shape. —Mark Vonnegut, *The Eden Express*

In the previous chapter, we mentioned that most of the progressive deterioration that schizophrenia can incur will take place within the first five to ten years after the individual has experienced the first psychotic episode. It is worth reiterating this point if only to emphasize its implicit recommendation: that early diagnosis and intervention at the first signs of the disease can help to prevent its worst effects over the long term.

In the case of teenagers with the illness, it will almost certainly fall to their parents to take the initial steps toward arranging for them to get this needed help, beginning with an evaluation by a qualified professional.

Early diagnosis and intervention at the first signs of the disease can help to prevent its worst effects over the long term.

Getting that first evaluation may not be easy, however, nor will the teen's treatment likely go without a hitch once he or she is diagnosed with the illness. Most people with schizophrenia do not willingly go for help at the first signs of the disease, possibly because they believe that their delusions or hallucinations are real and that they are in no need of psychiatric treatment. Even if they do go for help very early in the course of the disease, available therapies might or might not prove successful on the first try. Moreover, people who are only just beginning to experience early symptoms of schizophrenia may be very reluctant to take medications for sustained periods, in part because they have a limited awareness of the seriousness of their illness and may be sensitive to, and object to, the side effects of the drugs. In view of these possible obstacles, the adolescent's family, especially his or her parents, will need to be persistent, be it by taking the lead in getting the troubled teen evaluated or by maintaining vigilant support and advocating for the teen throughout the treatment process.

Treatment Providers: Who They Are and How to Find the Right Ones

Perhaps confusingly, psychiatric disorders are routinely treated by a variety of licensed professionals, and psychiatrists, psychologists, social workers, and nurses are all involved in the treatment of schizophrenia. In some states, nurse practitioners and clinical psychologists are licensed to prescribe medications, but in most instances, all nonmedical practitioners provide some form of therapy to people with schizophrenia, while psychiatrists oversee their medication regimens. At many hospitals and clinics, teams of professionals will work together to provide a range of services to patients.

Unfortunately, the task of finding a psychiatrist and/or team of mental health professionals skilled at diagnosing and treating schizophrenia is neither simple nor foolproof. E. Fuller Torrey, a psychiatrist who is widely viewed as a national expert on schizophrenia, believes that relatively few doctors in the United States know much about, or are particularly interested in, the disease. He strongly recommends that families searching for good therapeutic support for someone they suspect may have schizophrenia do so by reaching out to other families who have experience with the disease. As he notes in his book *Surviving Schizophrenia* (2001), families "can often provide a quick rundown of the local resources and save weeks of hunting and false starts."

Parents with experience in finding a helpful psychiatrist or team for their own children also recommend that as a first step you should call your local office of a national mental health organization for assistance and guidance. Such organizations as the National Alliance on Mental Illness (NAMI) or the National Mental Health Association (NMHA) should be able to help you in the following ways:

- They'll take your concerns seriously and not dismiss your child's symptoms as "simply teenage stuff"
- They can help you locate a mental health clinic or practitioner willing to work with people who have schizophrenia, and particularly with children and adolescents
- They can provide you with a support group to join

Look in the Resources section at the end of this book for information about how to get in touch with these and similar groups.

No matter how many satisfied customers a psychiatrist or other mental health professional may have, it is vitally important that you feel comfortable with him or her yourself. NAMI has put together the following list of relevant qualities that you should look for during your first interview with a treatment provider. He or she should

- Speak your language fluently
- Acknowledge that schizophrenia is a complex disease with many components, biological, chemical, and environmental
- Recognize that you and your family will be part of the treatment team
- Be interested in what you have to say and solicit your views and observations about your child's progress or lack thereof
- Be genuinely interested in helping your child, even at reduced rates or in less frequent visits

At the same time, according to NAMI, the provider should not

- Communicate the view that there is a special mystique in psychiatry and that parents and consumers cannot understand it
- Approach the treatment of schizophrenia with a one-therapy-fits-all attitude
- Refuse to see patients anywhere but in the office; the best therapist is one who will go where help is needed

Contacting a major academic medical center can also be very helpful, if you are fortunate enough to live near one.

Contacting a major academic medical center can also be very helpful, if you are fortunate enough to live near one. Such medical facilities are likely to have experts on staff who specialize in schizophrenia and who are up to date on the most recent developments in the field. These professionals can maintain a liaison with the treatment team in the community and be available for future consultations.

Psychopharmacology, or Treating With Medication

Antipsychotic Medication

The cornerstone of any treatment plan for schizophrenia is the use of medications to control symptoms. The drugs used to treat schizophrenia are usually referred to as *antipsychotics*, although they are also sometimes called *neuroleptics* or the old-fashioned term, *major tranquilizers*. The medications are most effective at reducing delusions, hallucinations, bizarre behavior, aggressive impulses, and thought disorders—the positive symptoms of schizophrenia. They are less effective in reducing the negative symptoms, such as apathy, emotionlessness, and social withdrawal. Most studies have demonstrated that the positive symptoms of about 70% of patients with schizophrenia will improve on antipsychotics, while 25% will improve only a little or not at all, and 5% will get worse.

Antipsychotic medications can be divided into two classes: first-generation antipsychotics, which have been available since the 1950s and are also referred to as typical or conventional antipsychotics; and second-generation, or atypical, antipsychotics, which are much newer (see Table 1). Any antipsychotic available between 1954, when chlorpromazine (Thorazine) was first introduced, and 1990, when clozapine (Clozaril) came on the market, is considered a first-generation medication. Although exactly how they work is unknown, it is thought that typical antipsychotics work by blocking certain dopamine receptors (D_2), while the atypical drugs are thought to block other dopamine receptors,

Table 1. Commonly Used Antipsychotic Medications

First-generation ("Typicals")		Second-generation ("Atypicals")	
Trade name	Generic or chemical name	Trade name	Generic or chemical name
Haldol	haloperidol	Abilify	aripiprazole
Mellaril	thioridazine	Clozaril	clozapine
Navane	thiothixene	Geodon	ziprasidone
Prolixin	fluphenazine	Risperdal	risperidone
Thorazine	chlorpromazine	Seroquel	quetiapine
		Zyprexa	olanzapine

Source: Physicians Desk Reference, 2004.

such as D_3 and D_4, in addition to serotonin and glutamate receptors, and are classified as serotonin/dopamine antagonists.

THE DOPAMINE HYPOTHESIS REVISITED
The neurochemical explanation of schizophrenia has been a subject of considerable debate. Because the earliest antipsychotic, chlorpromazine, was known to be a dopamine antagonist, and because it could be observed to control prominent symptoms of schizophrenia, the dopamine hypothesis was developed in 1977. The theory assumes that both schizophrenia and its psychotic symptoms, such as delusions and hallucinations, are caused by increased levels of dopamine in the brain. The dopamine theory was contradicted, however, once it became clear that the newer, atypical antipsychotics, which have an antiserotonergic as well as an antidopaminergic effect, work not so much by controlling dopamine as by blocking serotonin.

OTHER DIFFERENCES BETWEEN TYPICAL AND
ATYPICAL ANTIPSYCHOTICS
The chief difference between the two drug classes is the fact that certain serious side effects are commonly associated with

first-generation drugs but only rarely associated with the newer ones. Those side effects are known as extrapyramidal system-related effects (EPS), because they involve the extrapyramidal system, which connects parts of the brain and spinal cord and is largely concerned with regulating certain reflex muscular movements. The side effects include Parkinsonian-type symptoms (tremors and rigidity), and akathisia (an inability to stay still that leads to restless overactivity), among others. At higher doses, conventional antipsychotics, in addition to EPS, may precipitate in some patients "neuroleptic dysphoria," which is characterized by increased anxiety, hostility, and depression. For these reasons, the first-generation or typical antipsychotics have become unpopular with many patients, some of whom have campaigned against their use. The older drugs tend to be as effective as the newer ones, however, as well as less expensive, and some are available in generic form.

By contrast, with their arrival on the market in the 1990s, the second-generation, atypical antipsychotic medications almost immediately became the drug of choice for the treatment of schizophrenia. They too have their side effects, but they are preferred over the older drugs, especially for young people or those in the early stages of the illness, primarily because they are far less likely to produce EPS. As a group, they appear to work as well as the older drugs. Indeed, a recent study funded by National Institute of Mental Health compared first- and second-generation medications and showed them to be of similar effectiveness, although once again, the way any antipsychotic medication works against schizophrenia is still not fully understood.

Second-generation, atypical antipsychotic medications almost immediately became the drug of choice for the treatment of schizophrenia.

The oldest of the second-generation antipsychotics is clozapine (Clozaril), which is known to be effective in some cases where no other drug has worked. It is also the only antipsychotic that has been shown to be effective against negative symptoms (apathy, social withdrawal, and lack of emotion). Unfortunately, Clozaril is associated in rare instances with a life-threatening side effect, agranulocytosis, a disorder in which a deficiency of certain white blood cells is caused by damage done to bone marrow by the drug. Because of the risk of agranulocytosis, Clozaril is generally only used in cases where other drugs have not worked, and people who take it must have regular blood tests.

Since Clozaril came on the U.S. market in 1990, it has been joined by five other atypicals, each of which is considered effective in the treatment of schizophrenia. While every medication has potential side effects, none of the side effects is as disabling as untreated illness. Still, although most of the atypicals do not tend to cause EPS, several second-generation antipsychotics are likely to cause sedation and serious weight gain that may be associated with elevated blood sugar or even diabetes. There are also side effects associated more specifically with each individual medication.

It should be noted that some patients may respond well to one type of medication, such as a low-dose typical antipsychotic, while others may respond well to another type of medication, such as an atypical at the appropriate dose. Ultimately, the decisions about which medication is best should be individualized, and the use of multiple medications, without therapeutic benefit and with potential for increased side effects, should be avoided. Moreover, when any medication is prescribed for your child, it is essential that you discuss all aspects of the therapy with the psychiatrist providing the care, so that you understand the recommendation that is being made. Educating yourself about potential side effects and becoming actively engaged in the treatment process will help keep you informed and able to make the most of your child's care.

ADHERENCE WITH MEDICATION

Some, perhaps many, newly diagnosed patients may try to avoid taking medication of any sort, partly because they do not believe they are ill, but also because of irritating side effects, such as weight gain or dry mouth. Nonadherence (or "noncompliance," as refusal to take medication was once called) with oral antipsychotic therapy is estimated to be somewhere between 15% and 35% among hospitalized patients, and as high as 65% among outpatients. To counter this tendency of people with schizophrenia to stop taking their pills, several antipsychotics are available as long-acting injectables, including the typical antipsychotic fluphenazine (Prolixin) and the atypical risperidone (Risperdal). Nonadherence rates with the injectables are estimated at between 10% and 15% within two years, and 40% within seven years. Obviously, failure to go along with the therapeutic regimen significantly adds to a patient's risk of relapsing. Nevertheless, antipsychotics remain a mainstay of therapy for schizophrenia, and one of the primary goals of research in the field of psychiatry has been to find an antipsychotic able to suppress psychotic symptoms without producing undesirable side effects. Another goal is to develop medications that treat not only the positive symptoms but also the negative symptoms and the cognitive deficits (e.g., problems with attention or memory) associated with the illness.

Other Psychoactive Medications or Biological Approaches

Although the first choice of a drug to treat schizophrenia will almost certainly be an antipsychotic, other medications may also be used on occasion. Lithium, a natural salt used to treat bipolar disorder (manic depression), may be used in conjunction with an antipsychotic, to treat schizoaffective disorder or schizophrenia. Similarly, an antidepressant may be given to a patient who has schizophrenia with symptoms of depression as well, although the Food and Drug Administration (FDA) has issued a warning about the possible increased risk of suicidal behavior and thinking associated with the use of some antidepressants in young people, and has emphasized the need for careful monitoring of any children or adolescents who are taking these medications. Antiepileptic drugs (anticonvulsants) sometimes work for patients with schizophrenia, especially if they have abnormal brain waves as measured by electroencephalogram (EEG), but these drugs do not appear to be effective as maintenance therapy. Anti-anxiety drugs like diazepam (Valium) or chlordiazepoxide (Librium) may be helpful for some patients who are agitated or aggressive, although it should be noted that these medications have a serious potential for abuse and are not FDA-approved treatments for schizophrenia.

Electroconvulsive therapy, or ECT, is of genuine benefit to some people with severe depression who do not respond to antidepressant medication. It has not proved useful in the treatment of schizophrenia, however, and is therefore rarely used in this population, except for significant catatonia, a state of immobility that is sometimes seen in schizophrenia.

Behavioral and Psychological Therapies

There are many forms of interventions used to treat psychiatric disorders besides medication; these are often generalized as nonsomatic therapies, meaning that their target is the individual's psychology or behavior, rather than his or her physical state. Because the nonsomatic therapies involve interpersonal communication, they are often called "talk therapies." Here is a brief overview of a number of prominent approaches to psychiatric disorders that have been adapted for people who have schizophrenia

Because the nonsomatic therapies involve interpersonal communication, they are often called "talk therapies."

Supportive Psychotherapy

Supportive psychotherapy is intended to create a corrective emotional experience, thereby restoring and strengthening the patient's stability and developing healthy ways of solving problems. Combined with medications, a very mild form of supportive psychotherapy might be used to treat some people with schizophrenia. Some interest in a specific type of short-term psychotherapy called *interpersonal psychotherapy* (IPT), developed specifically to treat depression, has led to its experimental use in adults with schizophrenia by helping them address their dysfunctional interpersonal behavior.

Behavior Therapy

In behavior therapies, the focus of the treatment is on addressing maladaptive behaviors. Under the premise that all behavior is learned and therefore can be unlearned, behaviorists look for evidence of specific undesirable behaviors that have been learned or conditioned, with the goal of replacing them with desirable alternatives. Some hospitals, especially longer-term inpatient facilities, have used "token economy" procedures to teach social skills to patients with schizophrenia by rewarding good behaviors, such as participation in activities and self-care, and some evidence suggests that social skills training may be helpful for adolescents with the disorder.

Cognitive Therapy and Related Approaches

Cognitive therapy is a short-term structured therapy that focuses on very specific problems and seeks to resolve them through collaborative efforts between patient and therapist to improve the patient's "thinking skills." This form of therapy is chiefly used to treat depression, with the goal of helping patients change the negative ways they think about themselves. This therapy is not widely used to treat schizophrenia, although some researchers have begun to investigate the use of cognitive remediation therapy (CRT) to enhance therapeutic outcomes in adults with psychotic illnesses. Based on the extensive literature demonstrating the difficulties in attention, learning, and memory that those with the illness tend to experience, CRT training programs have focused on strengthening these cognitive abilities in patients, who in turn have shown improved performance as a result. Such efforts are promising avenues for intervention and apply principles that are used in remediation of other brain disorders.

Also, a combined form of cognitive and behavioral therapeutic techniques, cognitive-behavioral therapy (CBT), is increasingly used as part of a comprehensive therapy for schizophrenia that emphasizes social skills training. This mode of intervention is gaining interest among professionals and has been applied successfully in England in treating hallucinations and delusions.

Group Therapy

Group therapy, in which groups of people address interpersonal and life issues together under the guidance of a psychotherapist, is a natural setting for adolescents, who are usually more comfortable with, and more likely to be able to hear criticism from, their peers than they are from adults. However, group therapy can be damaging for fragile adolescents and for those with obvious symptoms or character traits likely to provoke ridicule from their peers. Some adolescents with schizophrenia might do well in group therapy, while others would not.

Family Therapy

Family therapy, in which entire families meet together with a psychotherapist, is the treatment of choice for adolescents whose problems are clearly the reflection of a dysfunctional family, such as teenagers who run away or avoid going to school. It may also be useful for families in which a teenage member has stirred up conflict within the family by trying to be independent. All family therapies seek to improve family conflicts through "psychoeducation," a procedure whereby families are taught better ways to interact with one another. Family therapy might be helpful for some families with a member who has schizophrenia, particularly if psychoeducation is at its core.

> *All family therapies seek to improve family conflicts through "psychoeducation," a procedure whereby families are taught better ways to interact with one another.*

Medication Plus Psychotherapy

Increasingly, researchers have reported that a combination of somatic and nonsomatic therapies work better than either alone in a variety of patient groups. In an unusual example of such research, a 2004 survey of 3,079 subscribers to *Consumer Reports* found that a combination of talk therapy and medication worked best by producing more improvement, though drugs worked faster to relieve symptoms. Some respondents reported that "mostly talk" therapy worked better than "mostly medication." Psychiatric journals have reported similar findings, beginning in 1996 with the revelation that 40% of patients do not fully overcome their symptoms with medication alone.

One research group has been actively studying what treatments help people with schizophrenia for some time, and they have discovered that a combination of medication and "psychosocial" interventions—therapies geared to the treatment of both psychological and social factors—are most effective at improving the patients' lives. Many elements of the nonsomatic therapies just covered here are mentioned in their reports, including psychoeducation, social skills training, family therapy, and elements of cognitive-behavioral therapy.

Hospitalization

The only child of an affluent family from the South, Emily was an academically gifted student who surprised no one when she was accepted to an elite university in the New York City area, where she planned to study biology. During her first semester, though, she stopped going to class or to meals, preferring to eat large quantities of snack food in her room. Her roommates became concerned about her and notified their residential advisor that something was wrong.

Because Emily was under 18, the school notified her parents, who flew to the school at once. By the time they arrived, she was in an infirmary at the student health service, where staff had established that she had been a heavy user of marijuana for years, a fact she had successfully kept hidden from her parents. More recently, she had developed a number of "troubling ideas," as the health service staff put it. "You may find Emily has changed a bit since you last saw her," a social worker said to her parents.

Emily had indeed changed. Disheveled and grubby, she had gained a good deal of weight and her clothes were too small and badly in need of laundering. She addressed her parents as "Your Majesties" while insisting that they remove her from "this torture chamber." Emily was suffering from delusions featuring the FBI and CIA, and was convinced that her father had stolen her formula for a smallpox vaccination.

The student health center helped Emily's parents arrange for her to be hospitalized in a program affiliated with the university's medical school, where she was diagnosed with schizophrenia and started on an atypical antipsychotic. After 30 days, Emily's delusional symptoms had diminished and her parents were able to take her home.

Most people with acute schizophrenia need to be hospitalized, and any person experiencing a first psychotic episode is acutely ill by definition. If you suspect that your child is developing schizophrenia, you will very likely need to arrange a hospital stay for him or her, as early in the disease course as possible. If you have the financial means, you may prefer a private institution, but if you are like most Americans, you will probably have to rely on the hospital that is approved by your insurance company or that is connected with your health maintenance organization (HMO). What is available to you will depend on your health insurance, but a typical insurance plan will provide the following, assuming eligibility requirements dictated by the insurance company have been met:

- 30 days of inpatient psychiatric services
- An additional 30 days may be available, provided the patient's medical team and the carrier agree that the case warrants it
- 60 days of inpatient services per year are usually the maximum benefit provided
- Each patient is subject to a maximum lifetime benefit ranging from $100,000 to $1 million, with substantial co-pay; most plans provide up to $500,000

Barrier to Mental Health Care: Affordability

The 2003 National Survey on Drug Use and Health (NSDUH) reports that the most formidable barrier keeping people from getting the care they need for serious mental illness is cost. The survey found that in a sample taken of the 5.9 million people with serious mental illness that did not seek treatment, nearly half blamed cost and/or insurance issues, while about 22% blamed the stigma of mental illness and 7% reported avoiding treatment out of fear of being committed or forced to take medication.

In hopes of addressing the insurance issues facing Americans with mental illnesses, Congress passed the Mental Health Parity Act in 1996. This Act was intended to remain in effect for six years, or until December 31, 2002, with the goal of making mental health benefits equal to those provided for medical and surgical illnesses. The Act was a federal law prohibiting group health plans from placing annual or lifetime dollar limits on mental health benefits that were lower than those the same plan offered for medical and surgical benefits. In other words, a health plan with a $1 million lifetime limit on medical benefits could not place a $100,000 lifetime limit on mental health benefits.

Although the Act had only a minimal cost, estimated to be about a 1.4% increase in premiums across the board, the American Public Health Association reports that fully 87% of insurance plans complied in a way that violated the spirit of the law, by replacing dollar limits with arbitrary limits on days spent in the hospital or the number of outpatient visits covered, not to mention raising copays. When the Act was about to expire, Congress failed to pass a new law on time, voting only to extend it one more year, through 2003. Advocacy groups such as the National Mental Health Association continue to urge Congress to pass legislation, which is now called the Paul Wellstone Mental Health Parity Act and has yet to become law.

In addition to the costs, you'll face other challenges, among them the limited criteria upon which hospital commitment may be justified. For many years, long-term, hospital-based residential treatment for schizophrenia was state-of-the-art. No longer. For many reasons, most of them financial and political, hospitalization today is used solely in the following instances:

- diagnosis and stabilization of medications
- for the safety of those patients thought to be either suicidal or homicidal
- for those patients who are so disorganized and bizarre that they are unable to take care of their most basic needs, like food, shelter, and personal hygiene

Ideally, hospital stays will be used to plan for a patient's life after he or she leaves—plans for housing, self-care, outpatient therapy, and school or work will all be put in place—and the patient and his or her family will be thoroughly educated about the disease and its care. While in the hospital, patients will use the relatively stress-free setting to learn how to structure their daily activities. Length of stay will depend on the severity of the patient's disorder, the available outpatient treatment settings, and the terms of the patient's insurance coverage.

> Ideally, hospital stays will be used to plan for a patient's life after he or she leaves.

That's the idea, anyway. In reality, hospitalization can be quite difficult to arrange, particularly if the person with schizophrenia does not believe there is anything wrong with him or her and has to be admitted involuntarily. Kate, the mother of a young man with schizophrenia, points out that to arrange an involuntary hospitalization in her community, it is necessary to call the local police. "First, you have to convince the police he's crazy. If you do that, which is not easy, then you have to convince EMT [emergency medical technicians, who staff the ambulance summoned by the police] he's crazy, which is even harder, and then you get to the hospital and you have to convince the admitting doctor he's crazy."

This procedure becomes vastly more complicated and difficult once the person with schizophrenia turns 18: "Parents lose their power when kids turn 18, because then the system closes down to parents," says Kate. In what seems like a classic catch-22, the adolescent with schizophrenia must live with his parents because he can't take care of himself, but if the parents think he needs to be in a hospital, he has to be willing to go or the police or EMT won't take him and the hospital won't admit him. Unfortunately, schizophrenia is a disease of remissions and relapses, and hospitalization will occasionally be necessary at times of particular stress and difficulty for the patient. Parents will need to develop the skills required to negotiate this process, because in all likelihood they will be called upon to use them every now and again.

What Parents Can Do

Parents can get all pertinent information in advance. For example, they can memorize the details of their health insurance plan. They can find out what the criteria for involuntary admission are in their state, along with the accepted procedures for commitment. Psychiatric hospital admission units and court clerks are usually knowledgeable in this area, as are local chapters of NAMI and state and local departments of mental health. Other important information to obtain is your state's definition of "dangerousness," often the key criterion used to decide if an individual may be hospitalized against his or her will. Is the individual eligible for involuntary admission in your state if he has threatened someone or only if he has actually injured someone? As E. Fuller Torrey points out, "many family members of people with schizophrenia end up becoming amateur lawyers in order to survive!"

Some parents may find their skills as "amateur lawyers" quite useful in another

"Many family members of people with schizophrenia end up becoming amateur lawyers in order to survive!"

forum: persuading their insurance companies to permit their child to remain in the hospital long enough to achieve some therapeutic success. Regardless of what you may be told by politicians and hospital administrators, insurance companies do indeed have a big voice in decision making, particularly as regards psychiatric admissions and discharges. Frank once spent the better part of two days on the phone with his insurance company with the goal of talking them into continuing the hospitalization of his son, diagnosed with schizophrenia, a mere two extra days, for a total of four. The insurance company had refused to authorize the extra days even though the patient maintained an openly messianic delusion that he had been "called" to embark upon a 40-day fast and walk through the desert. Frank ultimately prevailed by threatening to take his case to their state insurance commission, and recommends that all parents make it a point to learn the name and phone number of the group responsible for overseeing insurance companies in their states.

Outpatient Therapy

With hospital stays severely limited by the extent of patients' insurance coverage, the bulk of the treatment most people with schizophrenia will receive will be provided by outpatient facilities. Some communities are better served than others, and the quality and priorities of outpatient clinics can vary significantly. Even though no two treatment regimens will be exactly the same, all parents will probably need to be vigilant to make sure their child is getting adequate care after discharge from a hospital.

It used to be, some years ago, that the treatment of schizophrenia was considered successful if the patient was able to live outside a hospital and receive long-term treatment at an outpatient clinic. Now, however, the fact that most people with schizophrenia are expected as a matter of course to live in the community means that merely doing so is not a therapeutic outcome so much as it is an economic or political one. Rapid discharge from hospitals means that most, if not all, patients will continue to have symptoms and be somewhat disabled for some time after leaving the hospital, all of which points to a very important role for outpatient settings to fill.

Ideally, an outpatient clinic will assign each patient to a counselor or therapist able to provide ongoing, regular therapy or a combination of therapies geared to both psychological and social concerns. This kind of treatment is a practical, here-and-now approach to the problems of daily life, which can be quite daunting for people with schizophrenia. Topics that are likely to be covered in weekly visits should focus on how to improve the person's life, whether by training for and finding a job, making friends, or getting along better with his or her family. Psychologists and social workers are most likely to serve as patients' therapists, although psychiatrists may fulfill this function, as do nurses or other mental health professionals, such as rehabilitation counselors.

> Topics that are likely to be covered in weekly visits should focus on how to improve the person's life, whether by training for and finding a job, making friends, or getting along better with his or her family.

One would think, given the established effectiveness of outpatient counseling, that there would be an abundance of outpatient treatment available to those with schizophrenia. Such is not the case. It is a regrettable fact that many of the finest mental health clinics in the United States prefer not to make their desirable services available to people with schizophrenia. There are at least a few reasons for this prejudice. Therapists often prefer to work with lucid, insightful people—the "worried well"—because they tend to be more rewarding and less crisis-prone. Clinic administrators prefer to serve a population likely to generate positive outcomes that can be tallied and shown to regulators as proof that the clinic is earning its keep. The problem with these preferences lies of course in the unbalanced allocation of limited resources: If a clinic devotes most or all of its time to the "worried well," it will have no time or resources left for the seriously mentally ill. But that is what has happened in many mental health programs in the United States.

There is also a historical reason for the lack of outpatient services for the seriously mentally ill, including people with schizophrenia. In 1963, President John F. Kennedy signed the Community Mental Health Center Construction Act (PL 88-164), a federal initiative intended to provide grants for the building of community mental health centers (CMHCs), which were to provide comprehensive mental health centers across the country, especially to those who could not pay. The CMHC movement was born in a recognition that mental illness was much more common than had been thought, coupled with the idea that an enlightened society could eliminate psychiatric disorders by preventing them from developing in the first place. To accomplish these ambitious goals, the legislation required that each community provide inpatient, outpatient, partial hospitalization, emergency, and educational services, the chief goal of which was prevention of mental illness rather than care of the already mentally ill. While the CMHC model of psychiatric care seemed feasible in the 1960s, its agenda of prevention quickly proved incompatible with the needs of the worst-off psychiatric patients—the chronically mentally ill, as they were known then, or the seriously and persistently mentally ill, as they are known today. In many cases, the disease that such patients have is schizophrenia, and the CMHC movement effectively abandoned them.

Born in optimism and hope, the CMHC movement fizzled away quite rapidly over the next two decades, largely because the centers were never adequately funded. By the time managed care arrived, CMHCs had gone the way of the dinosaur, leaving for-profit outpatient clinics to pick up the most desirable portion of the caseload—the "worried well." Managed care organizations function to keep medical costs down by tying profits to patient outcomes, thereby applying a "business model" to health care in order to save money by cutting costs. In such a market, a long-term chronic disease like schizophrenia comes in a poor second to the more time-limited problems that confront the "worried well," legitimate though they may be. For managed care organizations, it is vastly more cost-effective to take care of mild depression among employed adults by providing short-term outpatient-based treatment than it is to work intensively with people who have schizophrenia, who are often unemployed, and who may require rehospitalization from time to time. Hospital stays are much more expensive than outpatient visits, as shown in Table 2, which is one reason managed

Table 2. Typical Costs of Psychiatric Care in 2004*

Inpatient services (may exclude some doctors' fees)	Outpatient services
$607-750 per day	• Scheduled: $180 per visit • Emergency: $250 per visit

*Figures used are for New York State, where costs are generally assumed to be about 125% of those of other states, except for Connecticut and New Jersey, whose costs are assumed to be around 120% of most states'.

care organizations seek to avoid paying for them. Another reason is that since managed care's profits are tied to costs, the organization will certainly not make any money by taking care of patients with schizophrenia who may require repeated hospitalizations throughout the course of their illness.

What Parents Can Do

The first thing you can do in looking for a suitable outpatient treatment program for an adolescent or young adult who has been diagnosed with schizophrenia is to call the NAMI or NMHA hotlines in your community. Barbara, the mother of a son with schizophrenia, says she cannot emphasize this too strongly. Having been involved for years in her local chapter of the Family Alliance, part of NAMI, she knows from vast experience that the people who answer the phones will know which clinics in a particular area are willing to work with people with the disease. Knowing this ahead of time can save a lot of time and stress.

Partial Hospitalization or Intensive Outpatient Treatment

Some psychiatric hospitals maintain "step-down" units, which provide a level of care that is slightly less than full-bore hospitalization but somewhat more intensive than once-a-week visits to an outpatient clinic. An example of such a unit would be a day hospital program providing service to patients a maximum of about six hours per day, five days per week. Such a program may be known as "partial hospitalization" or "intensive outpatient" treatment. While it costs less than a hospital stay, partial hospitalization is nevertheless rationed by insurance companies' notions of what they will and will not reimburse, and participation in such a program will not be open-ended—patients may be eligible for a maximum of six weeks' care or thereabouts. When Frank's insurance company refused to pay for his son to stay in a hospital more than five days, because they didn't believe he was a danger to himself, Frank was able to convince them to substitute intensive aftercare as a cost-effective alternative. Now, Frank says, he won't call the police to have his son hospitalized if he goes off his medication; he'll get his insurance company to agree on another stay in intensive aftercare instead, by reminding them that it's so much cheaper.

Continuity of Care

Parents can insist from the very start on establishing and maintaining continuity of care. An extremely valuable therapeutic tool for people with schizophrenia, the idea behind continuity of care is that a single person (or team) will be responsible for the psychiatric care of a patient, no matter where he or she goes within the community—to hospital X, or outpatient clinic Y, or psychosocial club Z. In her book *My Sister's Keeper* (1992), about her older sister Sally, who was diagnosed with schizophrenia at age 18, Margaret Moorman recounts the events that followed her mother's death, which left her responsible for Sally, even though they lived hundreds of miles apart. Moorman makes it clear that the only way she was able to manage was through the auspices of Rhonda, a social worker who had entered the case long before the mother's death and continued to be involved for years afterward. Rhonda helped Sally in a variety of ways, ranging from financial man-

Parents can insist from the very start on establishing and maintaining continuity of care.

agement to securing hospital admissions to assisting on moving day when Sally left her group home for her own apartment.

The essence of Rhonda's service was continuity: Whatever changed in Sally's life, Rhonda was always there. It is a kind of case management that requires sole dedication to the patient's needs, with case managers like Rhonda serving the patient's best interests and goals with an objectivity that parents of children with serious long-term mental disorders like schizophrenia may not have. Parents will always be emotionally involved in the lives of their children and as a result may not always be able to negotiate on their behalf, especially in those instances when the children's best interests may entail emotionally difficult decisions with regard to patient care. A professional like Rhonda can help to ease this process.

Few programs provide adequate continuity of care, but some states do provide a service called "case management" to eligible long-term patients. It is a good idea to begin early to look into the availability of such a service in your state or community. Programs that deliver continuity of care through case management or continuous treatment teamwork do not advertise their services, but they do exist. Be persistent in calling your state and local mental health department to find out how to take advantage of what is available. Your local chapters of NAMI and NMHA may also know what services you may be entitled to.

This continuing story about Emily, the girl who was diagnosed with schizophrenia during her first semester in college, illustrates how one family navigated the therapeutic challenges they faced:

> The big question for Emily and her parents was where she would go for therapy once she left the hospital in New York and was back home in a small southern city a thousand miles away. Emily's parents got as many recommendations as they could from staff at the

hospital, as well suggestions from their local NAMI chapter, accessing it via the chapter's website. NAMI also referred them to a clinic that was sponsored by a hospital in the area where the family lived, and Emily and her parents were interviewed by clinic staff the day after they arrived home. The staff—a social worker, an administrator, and a psychiatrist—were pleasant and accommodating, but the parents were shocked by the limited services available to them under their insurance plan. Emily was entitled to a maximum of 100 sessions per year, with the actual number dependent upon development of a suitable treatment plan. Visits to a social worker for counseling, a psychiatrist for medication, and any emergency appointments would all have to come out of the annual maximum. It occurred to Emily's parents that even two outpatient visits a week, at 45 minutes each, would not be enough to meet her needs.

Emily's parents decided to attend a meeting of a NAMI-sponsored support group for parents of adolescents with mental illness, where they hoped to get to know other parents in similar situations and learn from their experience. They soon became active in their local chapter, lobbying their state department of mental health for better outpatient treatment options for people with serious mental illnesses.

Other Therapeutic Options: Psychiatric Rehabilitation

". . . recovery casts a much wider spotlight on restoration of self-esteem and identity and on attaining meaningful roles in society."

An important development in the treatment of serious mental illnesses is the growing interest among professional organizations in the idea of "psychiatric rehabilitation"— that is, the idea that recovery inevitably depends more on improved social and vocational function than on symptom reduction through medication. Although recovery does not have a single agreed-upon definition, the surgeon general of the United

Tips for Parents by Parents:
Things We've Learned About Treatment

- Don't be discouraged if it takes weeks or even months for your child to get stabilized on medication. A lot of us look for improvement too soon, like one to two days. It takes a while.
- Even when kids have been stabilized on meds, they may get sicker at times of stress and need an adjustment of dosage. Parents need to anticipate stressful situations and keep an eye out for symptoms at those times.
- Never let yourself forget that your child may genuinely not realize he's sick, which is called "lack of insight." What helps is to encourage him to deal with specific symptoms, like insomnia, rather than trying to address the totality of schizophrenia.
- Stop looking for a long-term hospital where your child can get totally well. Only a few still exist, and they're expensive. Moreover, patients have the right to refuse to go.
- Don't give up on finding quality care. It's hard to find, especially if you don't have a lot of money, but you will eventually find the right treatment.
- Don't waste time with doctors or therapists who refuse to work with you as well as your child. If they don't want your input, go to someone else.
- Don't be afraid to tell doctors what you know from experience won't work.

States has said that "the overarching message is that hope and restoration of a meaningful life are possible, despite serious mental illness. Instead of focusing primarily on symptom relief, as the medical model dictates, recovery casts a much wider spotlight on restoration of self-esteem and identity and on attaining meaningful roles in society."

As psychiatric patients and their parents are painfully aware, merely visiting a clinic every few weeks to get a prescription refilled for an atypical antipsychotic is not much of a life for any person with schizophrenia, least of all one who is newly diagnosed. What people with serious mental illnesses need just as much as medication is something to do in the daytime that will ultimately lead to their recovery. Just like people who do not have schizophrenia, the newly diagnosed teenager needs to acquire the skills and credentials necessary to enter the adult workforce, which means finishing school, building a work history, and developing social skills, in addition to learning how to live with the illness.

The principles of psychiatric rehabilitation were outlined by psychiatrist Stephen Marder in a talk entitled "Recovery in Schizophrenia" at a conference sponsored by the American Psychiatric Association in October 2004. Dr. Marder defined recovery as a process rather than a goal, one that people continue to work at regardless of the stage of illness they happen to be in. Whether an individual is symptomatic, asymptomatic, in remission, or in relapse, the focus of his or her treatment should be functional outcome rather than merely the relief of symptoms like delusions and hallucinations. Noting that at the time he spoke, only about 20% of people with schizophrenia were working at any job whatsoever, Dr. Marder criticized psychiatry for overemphasizing treatment of patients' symptoms with medication at the expense of their social and vocational function. "People can recover who have symptoms; people can work who experience hallucinations and have suspicious thoughts, just as people can recover and prosper if they are missing a limb. . . . Patients and families are asking for a recovery model [of therapy], and we need to respond."

Psychiatric rehabilitation programs (also called psychosocial rehabilitation programs) that are known to be effective in enabling recovery in people with schizophrenia generally include the following components, each of which can be expected to affect a different aspect of the illness:

- *Illness education*, in which patients learn what it is they have and what handicaps they can expect as a result, in addition to learning suitable coping skills that will enable them to function throughout all stages of the illness
- *Family interventions*, in which family members and patients learn how to live with one another and how best to manage disruptive aspects of the illness
- *Supported employment*, in which people with schizophrenia are given the chance to learn how to function in a job while working at it—through internships, for example
- *Social skills training*, in which people with schizophrenia learn how to interact with other people who may or may not know they have an illness
- *Cognitive-behavioral therapy* (CBT), a form of psychotherapy in which patients learn to replace self-defeating attitudes ("I'm hopeless; I'll never get a job") with more adaptive ones ("I am working out a plan to help me learn how to look for a job"); CBT teaches both management skills for anger, anxiety, and stress and social skills.

In the psychiatric rehabilitation model of treatment for schizophrenia, all of the above therapies are combined with appropriate medication for symptom management, as determined by the goals set by the individual patient for his own recovery. "Patients need to be at the center and be active partners in setting goals of treatment," said Dr. Marder. Recovery is a long-range process, if not a life-long one, and the effects of psychosocial therapies may not be seen in the short-term. It takes time to learn how to act on the job or at a

Recovery is a long-range process, if not a life-long one, and the effects of psychosocial therapies may not be seen in the short-term.

party, particularly if you are someone who has to suppress your "voices" at the same time. Most important of all is work: "No treatment I have seen is as effective as a part-time job," commented Dr. Marder. "Nothing contributes as much to self-esteem and community integration than being able to interact with co-workers on a regular basis, and there is nothing more reinforcing to a patient than being given a positive review by a supervisor and being paid for one's work."

Assertive Community Treatment

One rehabilitation-oriented approach to serious mental illness, and one that has engaged the attention of state and federal bureaucracies, is known as Assertive Community Treatment (ACT) or Program of Assertive Community Treatment (PACT). ACT is intended to keep patients with serious mental illness out of hospitals so that they can lead lives that are not dominated by mental illness. To do this, teams are assembled of the usual complement of mental health professionals with the addition of job counselors and substance abuse specialists, all of whom work together with small caseloads that they share. All treatment is done in the community—at patients' homes, at their job sites, and even jails and homeless shelters. Services are available 24 hours a day, 7 days a week, and as many times per day as the patient requires, and ACT programs are fully available to families as well.

ACT was started in Wisconsin and has been adopted by a number of other states, in large part because studies have determined that it is effective—people get better, which is usually measured in terms of whether they relapse and need to be rehospitalized. The ACT model of community treatment is considered an evidence-based service, or EBS, which means that state and federal governments will spend money on it. ACT has received the enthusiastic endorsement of NAMI and is described in glowing terms on their national website. ACT programs may be better suited to older patients, with more extensive histories of hospitalization and failed treatments of all kinds, than to teenagers. Moreover, it is still fairly new and programs do not as yet exist everywhere. See Appendix 2 for a list of states that provide ACT services.

Jump Start: A Model Psychiatric Rehabilitation Program

Located in Boston, Massachusetts, Jump Start was a career development and mentoring program developed in 2002 for young adults aged 16 to 26 with psychiatric disabilities, including schizophrenia, whose needs had long been overlooked by traditional mental health providers, with their emphasis on symptom control. Many of them had also "aged out" of the children's mental health system, losing that system's support in the process. Jump Start was designed to help these young people gain the skills, self-confidence, and education needed to transition effectively from school to independence through high-quality employment or college or both. The program had three special qualities:

- Unlike "therapy groups" held in a "clinic," Jump Start's classes were held on a college campus, which appealed to young participants discouraged by the stigma of mental illness that a clinic setting can exacerbate.
- Its students were encouraged to consider career options that inspired and excited them, rather than to settle for minimum-wage jobs in dispiriting environments.
- All students were assigned to mentors, adults with desirable jobs in the community who were themselves living with psychiatric disabilities. These mentors included people working in law, business, research, human services, and the arts.

The goal of Jump Start was to foster hope, trust, self-confidence, and self-efficacy in their students by providing them with the identical "normal" life experiences of their peers—finishing school, finding a job, making friends, performing basic tasks like shopping or doing laundry. With the support of their mentors, students chose semester-long classes designed to teach them skills they would need to facilitate their career development, including computer classes and GED (graduate equivalency diploma) classes leading to a high school diploma. Students, staff, and mentors planned outings and events designed to promote self-esteem and underscore the importance of participating in normal activities in life, even for people with serious mental illness. Such activities included hikes, benefit walks, volunteer work at a food bank, and attendance at sporting events.

Among the most important lessons that its designers learned was that Jump Start was desperately needed, and Alexandra Bowers, M.P.H., M.S.W., one of Jump Start's managers, continues to receive telephone calls from parents looking for a similar program for their children. Bowers says that what worked in Jump Start was its anchor in real life—the college setting, the concrete lessons in resume writing, interviewing, and basic computer skills, the internships and long-range career planning. The mentor program was a most effective asset: The mentors, who had themselves learned to live productive lives in spite of psychiatric disability, were able to offer their charges realistic help and support as they learned how to solve problems that are especially challenging for people

> The mentors . . . were able to offer their charges realistic help and support as they learned how to solve problems that are especially challenging for people with mental illness.

with mental illness, such as how to avoid substance abuse and risky sexual activity. The mentors were also able, from their own experience, to deflect participants from self-defeating rebelliousness that led to nonadherence with treatment.

Sadly, despite its proven success and positive feedback from program auditors, Jump Start was unable to secure ongoing funding beyond its single year as a pilot program. In the end, continued funding was denied on the grounds that the program addressed only a single disability—psychiatric illness—and was therefore not universally available to all disabled individuals. But what is important to emphasize here is that the program did exist, it did work, and it has established a model that others can follow in developing effective programs oriented toward recovery rather than settling for just symptom relief in young people with schizophrenia.

Other Model Rehabilitation Programs in the United States

A few programs around the country provide psychosocial rehabilitation services of some sort to people with serious mental illnesses, including schizophrenia. When you are looking within your own state for such programs, it may be a good idea to mention the following programs as examples of the kind of treatment you are looking for:

- *California: The Village* (www.village-isa.org). The Village Integrated Service Agency is a program operated by the Mental Health Association of Los Angeles. It provides a rich range of services to people with schizophrenia and was established through a statewide competition calling for an integrated service delivery system based on a particular kind of funding. Its goal is to enable participants to "live, learn, socialize, and work in the community," through self-help, family support, peer support, and community involvement; all members are encouraged to work and are supported on the job by personal service coordinators. The program saves money by providing treatment in the community, thereby cutting down on the need for expensive hospitalizations.

- *Michigan: The Michigan Supported Education Program* (www.ssw.umich.edu/sed/). The origin of this program was a research demonstration project designed to serve adults with psychiatric disabilities in the Detroit area. The program operated successfully on two college campuses, in Detroit and Dearborn, enabling adults with serious mental illness to prepare to matriculate at local community colleges and to work toward career and educational goals they had chosen. The program offered classes designed to provide students with the academic and social skills necessary to achieve their goals; topics included coping with the academic environment and stress management. Instead of being mental patients, participants were considered students and were treated as such. Like Jump Start, the Michigan program lost its funding and has had to close. "Unfortunately, although the empirical evidence for supported education is growing, only a handful of psychiatric rehabilitation agencies have adopted this technology," regret the program's designers. In spite of losing their funding, the people involved in the project remain convinced of its value and hope to continue with their mission, and they will provide advice to interested consumers.

- *Southern New England: Vinfen* (www.vinfen.org). Vinfen is a private, not-for-profit human service organization providing housing and other services to people with psychiatric disabilities in New England since 1977. Services include supported apartment living, specialized residential facilities for people with HIV/AIDS or substance abuse problems, and group living settings for people who have a high need for staff support. Vinfen augments their housing programs with clubhouse services, outpatient and emergency treatment, day and employment services, crisis respite services, peer support, psychosocial education, and community outreach.

You will find addresses, phone numbers, and profiles of these and other psychiatric rehabilitation programs in the Resources section of this book.

Work-Oriented Treatment Programs

A number of ex-patients, or consumers, have developed therapeutic approaches to serious mental illness based on the idea that most patients' lives are entirely dominated by their illnesses and that they are passive recipients of endless services that get them nowhere. The essence of the advocates' alternative approach involves peer support coupled with opportunities to work productively. While such programs are important for underscoring the fact that a diagnosis of schizophrenia need not be a life sentence, they are probably more useful for longtime patients than for those who are still in their adolescence and not yet in the work force. They also tend to be unique and available only to residents of their founders' communities.

The advocates' alternative approach involves peer support coupled with opportunities to work productively.

The idea that people with serious mental illness can and should work in regular jobs has led to a fairly large-scale deployment of programs of supported employment. Like the ACT programs, supported employment is considered an evidence-based service (EBS), so federal and state governments are funding it, which is what "supported" means. Supported employment programs will help people with mental illness find and keep real jobs. As of 2003, a survey found that 42 states had implemented supported employment programs. See Appendix 2 for a breakdown of states to see if yours provides supported employment services.

Fountain House: The Clubhouse Model

Dissatisfied with the very limited options for therapy for serious mental illness dictated by insurance companies and eager to prove that people with schizophrenia really can get better, several ex-patient activists have developed alternatives. Among the best-known is Fountain House, a club for discharged psychiatric patients that was founded in 1948 by a small group of people who had been discharged from a mental hospital run by New York State. Today, members of the club can visit the program any day of the year to take advantage of opportunities to work within the program, to be entertained, or to learn more about themselves and the world they live in. Key to the Fountain House model is the deliberate choice of the words "club" and "clubhouse" rather than therapy program: Fountain House is intended to be more like a private home than a treatment center.

The original clubhouse has grown to include housing and even a working farm, staffed by members. It also sponsors a young-adult program that is focused on helping young people between the ages of 16 and 30 to finish school, manage activities of daily living, acquire social skills, learn job skills, find housing, and so on.

Fountain House is unquestionably a success in many ways, having spawned an international clubhouse movement and many imitators. There are limitations to its access, however: for example, applicants must be "clean and sober"—that is, not abusing substances—for at least 60 days before they can join.

Adherence: Getting the Most Out of Treatment

Clearly, the best treatment for schizophrenia will be one that prevents or at least postpones relapse into psychosis. Fortunately, younger patients, in their teens or twenties, are generally very responsive to therapy, and most of them can overcome their early psychotic symptoms entirely. The next goal of therapy will be to achieve the best possible functional recovery, meaning restoration to as normal a life as possible—such as returning to school or to work. What will generally be required to achieve recovery will be medication, ongoing counseling that includes extensive education about schizophrenia, and lots and lots of support from therapists, family, and friends. It will not be easy for the individual to go back to school or work after a psychotic episode, but with a combination of assistance, he or she can and will be ready to do so in time. Frank's son, for example, had his first psychotic break at 16 and missed a great deal of school, but he was able to go back and finish a year or so later.

For any treatment plan to work, it is necessary for the patient to adhere to its requirements, such as showing up for appointments with therapists on time or taking medication as prescribed. This is sometimes easier said than done, however. As noted previously, for example, many patients stop taking their medication because of unpleasant side effects. Other reasons for such lack of adherence with treatment may include the following:

- Because of brain injury or damage, the person is unaware that he or she is sick. Called anosognosia, this lack of awareness that anything is wrong is also seen in people with other brain disorders.
- Denial: The person is aware of being sick but refuses to admit it. Having to take medicine or go see a doctor only reminds him or her of the illness, whereas not taking any medication suggests that nothing is wrong.
- Poor doctor-patient follow-up: Many outpatient programs only allow for psychiatrists to spend about 15 minutes per patient, four to six times a year, to follow up on medication, which is hardly enough time to discuss side effects, much less form a relationship.
- Delusions: "Medication is poison and people are using it to kill me," or "I am king of the world and only have to do what I want," or "God told me not to take any pills" are all examples of common delusions that interfere with the taking of medication.
- Confusion, disorganization, and a fear of becoming addicted can also contribute to patients' nonadherence with medication.

Ian Chovil, an individual with schizophrenia whose website (www.chovil.com) describes his own personal experience with the illness, identifies other reasons for nonadherence:

- Mental illness by definition causes disability. Some people with mental illness follow the advice given to them by the "voices" they hear in their heads, don't realize they are mentally ill, and never think of taking medication.
- Adherence with medication interferes in recreational drug use.

- For young people, the idea of taking medication for a long time and maybe for much of their lives is very scary.
- Some people like their symptoms. Delusions and hallucinations may support the attractive idea that they are very special. Medication will take that specialness away.
- Some people think having to take medicine is a sign of inferiority or weakness.

What Parents Can Do

Parents can take an active role in helping their children adhere to the requirements of their medication by first learning as much as they can about the medication itself and its role in the treatment of schizophrenia. They can encourage their children to learn about it as well. They should also develop strategies for addressing the reasons their children may give for not taking their meds. One such strategy is to explain to your child that the disease of schizophrenia is not unlike other medical conditions, such as diabetes or hypertension. One father, for example, finds it helpful to remind his daughter that antipsychotic medication, for her, is like insulin for a diabetic, or an inhaler for an asthmatic, and that

One father . . . finds it helpful to remind his daughter that antipsychotic medication, for her, is like insulin for a diabetic, or an inhaler for an asthmatic.

having to take medication should not be viewed as a limitation of personal freedom or a sign of personal inferiority but a therapeutic intervention.

Another strategy is to set useful limits. Frank, the father of a boy with schizophrenia, also has a brother with the disease. Because his brother has always refused to take any medication for schizophrenia, with predictably negative results, Frank was determined to see his son take a different course. The son is reasonable and pleasant as long as he takes his medication, but once he stops, he develops messianic delusions and focuses on his "call" to fast and walk in the desert for 40 days. Frank has developed an effective strategy for those occasions when his son stops taking his meds: He arranges for a return to intensive outpatient treatment the minute he realizes a dose or more has been missed, thereby avoiding having to call the police and force his son into a hospital against his will. Frank feels comfortable making it clear to his son that if he does not go along with this plan, he will call the police and the son will go into a hospital. Much the same approach occurred with Emily:

> Emily went to see her new psychiatrist and social worker twice before deciding they were "agents of the government sent to keep tabs on [her]." She apparently decided that the medications that had been prescribed for her were intended to prevent her from completing her self-appointed research tasks and stopped taking them right away, lying about it to her worried parents. Because the outpatient visits took up so little of her time, she quickly lapsed into the behavior noted by her college roommates: She slept most of the day, watched a lot of TV, and avoided interactions with her family.
>
> After a month of this, Emily's parents worked with the clinic staff to get her assigned to their partial hospitalization program and told her she could either comply with that routine or they would call the police and have her rehospitalized. Emily grudgingly agreed to go to the clinic program, where she stayed for about six weeks.

Treating Associated Problems

Substance Abuse

Marijuana, or cannabis, is by far the most common illicit substance used by adolescents in this country. Known colloquially by many names—pot, weed, grass, ganja, hemp, and dagga are a few—marijuana is used by about 5% of the U.S. population over 12, and over 8% of all kids aged 12 to 17. Among adolescents with schizophrenia, however, marijuana use is much more common—about 15% to 20%. Cannabis is smoked for its euphoric effects, which appear in minutes, peak in about 30 minutes, and last two to four hours. Although it rarely causes a bad-trip experience of the sort associated with hallucinogens such as LSD, peyote, or "'shrooms," it can induce paranoid thinking that is usually transient. It is these effects—euphoria and psychoticlike thinking—that can appeal to adolescents who are developing schizophrenia, simply because they provide an explanation for their symptoms, even as they temporarily relieve them.

There is no doubt that teenagers with schizophrenia commonly turn to marijuana and alcohol to help them cope with their disease—all of the parents interviewed for this book reported that their children had used large amounts of marijuana or hallucinogens shortly before their first psychotic episode. And there is little doubt that smoking pot has a negative effect on people at risk for schizophrenia: marijuana use, especially early in life, increases the risk of developing symptoms of the disease, and it is likely that continued use of marijuana by teenagers with schizophrenia will make them worse instead of better. Use of the substance may also become heavy and chronic.

Apart from special "Mentally Ill Chemical Abuser" (MICA) programs, which are intended to treat people who are both substance abusers and seriously mentally ill, there are relatively few treatment options for people with schizophrenia who are also severe substance abusers. Because they carry two diagnoses, they may get caught up in the regrettable specialization that permeates the mental health industry. A patient may be shuttled between a psychiatric program that will serve the mentally ill—but not if they abuse substances, because drugs and alcohol supposedly interfere with the treatment—and a drug treatment program that will have nothing to do with people with schizophrenia, on the grounds that the staff are not expert in their care. When that happens, inevitably the patient is the one to suffer.

One family found this out the hard way, when looking for a treatment program for a member with alcoholism and schizophrenia:

> Believing these disorders to be interrelated, we made every effort to find a program that would focus on both disorders at once, rather than one at a time. There was nothing out there. Each year, thousands of families struggle to find dual-disorder treatment—most without any luck.

Their solution was to found their own program, WestBridge, "a private non-profit organization dedicated to supporting the recovery of families and individuals who experience co-occurring mental illness and substance use disorders." The WestBridge program, which is oriented to people in their twenties, includes respite care, case management, and residential support, all of it delivered with a strong emphasis on the role of the family in supporting recovery. The essence of WestBridge's approach is the provision of mental health and substance abuse services together, in one place and at the same time, tailored to the individual and the stage of recovery he or she is in. Like Jump Start, WestBridge is located in the Boston area. "This is a great organization for anyone who gets sick in college in Boston—it is very recovery-oriented and has lots of services," commented Alexandra Bowers, of the Boston University Center for Psychiatric Rehabilitation.

The WestBridge model of dual-disorder treatment has expanded to New Hampshire, through a partnership between the

West Institute and the New Hampshire-Dartmouth Psychiatric Research Center. The New Hampshire organization is recovery-oriented and is invested in the study of psychosocial treatments such as supported employment, family psychoeducation, and illness management, in addition to the treatment of dual disorders, which they call "integrated dual disorders treatment." WestBridge opened its newest residential center in Manchester, New Hampshire, in the spring of 2005.

WHAT PARENTS CAN DO

The risk of developing chronic substance abuse in addition to mental illness is yet another reason why the early identification of schizophrenia is essential. It is important that you bear in mind the fact that cannabis and, to a lesser extent, alcohol, offer a reassuring excuse for symptoms that are frightening to someone experiencing them for the first time. Hearing voices telling you what to do or criticizing you in harsh terms would be unsettling to anyone, but even more so to a teenager who is struggling with normal issues of identity to begin with. Smoking a few joints can help, for the moment, by inducing euphoria, as well as by explaining the symptoms away. Nevertheless, for teenagers with schizophrenia, no illicit drug is a good idea. Marijuana can induce psychotic symptoms in anyone, which is obviously a bad thing in someone at risk for psychosis. Amphetamines, angel dust (PCP, or phencyclidine), special K (ketamine), and LSD are all drugs that should never be used by people with schizophrenia, because they are fully

> Hearing voices telling you what to do or criticizing you in harsh terms would be unsettling to anyone, but even more so to a teenager who is struggling with normal issues of identity to begin with.

capable of inducing psychosis. Parents should discourage their use absolutely.

Suicidal Behavior

One of the most frightening prospects for any parent is the possibility of suicide. As noted earlier, 30% of people with schizophrenia try to kill themselves at one time or another, and some do in fact die by suicide. Not all suicidal behavior is overt, however: It may be manifested in subtle ways, as when the individual contemplating suicide starts giving away possessions or writing a will, for example. If your teen acts or talks in a way that leads you to believe that he or she might be feeling suicidal, it is important that you act immediately. The following are some general principles to follow in a crisis involving suicide threats or attempts:

- Don't ignore talk about suicide; ask "Are you serious?" and "How can I help?"

Who Is at Risk for Suicide?

- People who have tried it before
- People who have talked about it before
- People who are anxious, depressed, and exhausted
- People with ready access to lethal weapons and toxic substances
- People who have talked about wanting to die
- People who have all of a sudden prepared a will or given their treasures away
- People who are in mourning or are facing a crisis
- People who act and seem as if they think things are hopeless
- People with a family history of suicide

- Take any attempt seriously
- Find out everything you can about the attempt—if pills were swallowed, for instance, find out how many and what they were
- Do not try to handle this alone! Get help immediately: Depending on the nature of the attempt, call your doctor, your child's doctor, Poison Control, or 911 for an ambulance
- Call the National Hopeline Network at 1-800-SUICIDE (784-2433)

Navigating the Health Care System

No parent with a child with schizophrenia can possibly manage without extensive knowledge of how to navigate the health care system. These are some tips from parents who have learned from experience:

- Know what your insurance covers and doesn't cover.
- Don't be surprised to find you have to fight with your insurance company to get the service your child needs, and don't shrink from the fight—the squeaky wheel gets the grease.
- Find out what psychiatric services are available in your community; be prepared to demand what your child needs.

  Be prepared to demand what your child needs.

- Learn the names and locations of government agencies that oversee psychiatric facilities and insurance companies; do not hesitate to call direct if you are not getting the care your child needs.

- Be prepared to have to convince police, EMS workers, and admitting psychiatrists that your son or daughter really is psychotic.
- Find out how your state defines "dangerousness" in a psychiatric patient.
- Learn the terminology of psychiatry and use it!
- Learn the language of the insurance company and use it!

Chapter Four

Everyday Life

Schizophrenia is an extremely guilt-provoking disease. It often strikes promising, gentle, bright young people, and the rapid changes into incoherency and vicious rejection are almost impossible to understand. The acceptance that it is a disease is the only positive first step.

—Elizabeth Swados, *The Four of Us: A Family Memoir*

Parents who live with mentally ill children have an extremely tough row to hoe. Not only do they have to put aside their hopes and expectations for what that person could have become, had things been different, but they must also cope with unnerving and even deranged behavior that other people may never see in their lives. They must spend hours, days, weeks— whatever it takes—tracking down therapists, hospitals, clinics, and favorable decisions from insurance companies. What is not always fully appreciated, however, is that the relatives of the mentally ill must also master their own emotional responses to the daily reminder that their son or sister is different, odd, peculiar, eccentric, unpredictable, and/or downright hostile. Finally, like their mentally ill relatives, they must endure the stigma attached to the condition.

Schizophrenia affects everyone connected with it—patient, family, and friends—and it places particularly onerous demands on the people closest to it.

While it may seem natural and right always to put first the person with the mental illness—schizophrenia, in this case—the truth is that parents need to take care of themselves in order to do the best possible job of taking care of a child with the disorder. Schizophrenia affects everyone connected with it—patient, family, and friends—and it places particularly onerous demands on the people closest to it. This is especially true for parents, who are the first line of defense against the disorder and the ones who must bear the brunt of much of the essential work involved, from coping with doctors, pharmacies, and insurance companies to answering questions from well-meaning friends and relatives. We will start, then, with the impact of schizophrenia on parents themselves.

Dealing With Your Own Feelings

The first thing to do is to face squarely what it is you are up against. Schizophrenia is not a benign condition. The people who have the illness are subject to irrational ideas and beliefs that are not shared by others, and they sometimes act upon those ideas in unexpected ways. Much of their behavior is strange or even bizarre—wearing red clothes exclusively, laughing with invisible companions, or signaling to unseen others out the window—and on occasion it may be dangerous, whether to property, to themselves, or to others.

For parents, living with an adolescent whose behavior is unpredictable will take a toll. The need to be vigilant is tiring, and living in suspense is exhausting. Kate, a psychologist and mother of a son with schizophrenia, makes the startling observation that "most people tend to romanticize the idea of family, of 'loved ones.' But we know that these kids drive their parents cuckoo—they're irrational and nonstop demanding. What people not in this situation don't realize is the way we live, the fact that we need to sleep with a [baseball] bat under the bed or have a stun gun in the house." Kate's comments will not come as a surprise to parents who have been in a situation in which a beloved child is turned by schizophrenia into a bundle of rage, capable of threatening behavior directed toward whoever may happen to be nearby.

Another enervating emotional reaction parents must be prepared to deal with is grief. The child they brought into the world is gone, replaced by someone who sometimes makes no sense. A familiar personality has been replaced with a mysterious other, someone with peculiar ideas and weird habits. The impact of this situation on parents cannot be exaggerated: They have sustained a loss that is unfair, undeserved, and relatively unusual, yet one that has dramatically changed their lives. Parents must expect to grieve, feeling much as they would had their son or daughter died. Barbara, the mother of a son with schizophrenia, remembers that *Parents must expect to grieve.* early on in his illness, she felt she was "the walking dead; it was like I was living on the edge of a grave." Another mother put it this way: "Words cannot describe what it's like. [These kids] die but they never get buried. Then they come back for a while, but you lose them again. And you think, "I can't go through this again.""

Parents will also likely feel tremendous guilt—about having somehow caused this illness in their children, about not initially recognizing or understanding its effects, and about not reacting as well as they would have preferred to their children's behavior.

As Anne Deveson writes in her memoir, *Tell Me I'm Here:*

> Doctors go out of their way to convince you that you are not to blame. Okay, so you listen to them, but deep down you have guilts that nobody knows about. You recall experiences when you yelled at your son—ah, like once when I said, "When are you going to draw something worthwhile, instead of cartoons all the time?" God, do I hate myself when I recall that feeling. Probably lots of parents yell at their children but for me I have that guilt.

Feeling Better: Advice for Parents From Parents

- **Know it's not your fault.** This is a disease that has nothing to do with your parenting.
- **Know it's not a character flaw.** Sometimes parents, especially fathers, feel embarrassed by the behavior of their children with schizophrenia and wish they would control themselves, which they can't. Your child is not acting strangely on purpose. He or she can't help it; your child's brain simply isn't working properly.
- **Learn everything you can about the illness.** It will help you handle your own feelings if you understand what is going on in your child. The important thing is to be there for your child when he or she needs you, helping in any way you legitimately can.
- **Don't hide the illness:** Use what you learn about it to educate others, just as the parents who helped in the preparation of this book have done.
- **Be prepared for relapse.** Prepare for the possibility that your child will relapse by finding out who on your local police force handles psychiatric emergencies—sometimes police departments have special community officers or community liaison people who can help you ahead of time,

so you'll know what to do in a crisis. Learn the local hospital's admission procedures, for the same reason. Develop a treatment team, starting with yourself, your spouse or significant other, friends, clergy, other parents you meet at NAMI—anyone you can trust to be helpful.

- **Don't be fooled by a "flight into health."** Schizophrenia is a chronic condition in the course of which acute episodes will recur from time to time. Enjoy the good days with your child whenever they occur, but don't assume the illness is gone, because it probably isn't.
- **Make time for your other children.** When a parent is faced with a demanding challenge like learning to manage a child who has been diagnosed with schizophrenia, it is easy to get so caught up in meeting the challenge that the parent forgets his or her other responsibilities. Your other children need you, too!
- **In addition to getting help for your child, seek help for yourself.** For example, get involved in a support group for parents of children with mental illness (see the discussion about support groups later in this chapter), or consider seeing a therapist yourself to help you cope with your feelings.

Dealing With the Stigma of Mental Illness

It is impossible to overestimate the impact of the general disregard in which most people in our culture hold the mentally ill. As Rebecca Woolis, author of *When Someone You Love Has a Mental Illness* (1992), has written:

> The lives of people with mental illness are made much more difficult by the fact that most people do not understand them. Most often

they are feared, avoided, or mocked. The alienation, isolation, and depression they feel as a result of these attitudes become secondary symptoms of the illness and make their lives more painful.

The same may be said for the families of the mentally ill, who must endure people who stare at, criticize, or make fun of their son or daughter, their brother or sister. In some ways, coping with the fact that the general public is both uninformed and intolerant of people with schizophrenia may be the hardest task faced by parents. As recently as the 1980s, a shocking proportion of people believed, for example, that schizophrenia is the same thing as multiple personality, and that severe mental illnesses were the result of patients' sins or weakness of character. One 1986 poll found that over half the public did not even believe such a thing as mental illness existed. Such confused and contradictory patterns of belief suggest that in spite of well-publicized research findings to the contrary, many or most people were basing their assumptions about the mentally ill on outdated stereotypes.

> Coping with the fact that the general public is both uninformed and intolerant of people with schizophrenia may be the hardest task faced by parents.

And unfortunately, one particular stereotype refuses to go away—that of the Dangerous Other. One of the stated goals of the practice of deinstitutionalizing the mentally ill, beginning in the mid-1950s, was the elimination of this particular stigma—the idea being that if mentally ill people were allowed to live in the community instead of in state mental hospitals, everyone would see them around and know they were just like the rest of us—but the truth is that the stigma is even stronger today than ever before. In 1999, the United States Surgeon General wondered why this stigma persisted despite better un-

Are People With Schizophrenia Violent?

Even though movies and TV like to connect criminal violence with mental illness, most people with schizophrenia are not particularly violent, and it is unusual for them to strike out at others. One estimate is that 4% of violent acts are committed by people with schizophrenia, and the incidence of homicide by those with the disease is even rarer—less than 1 in 3,000 cases. When such violent behavior does occur, it is generally in response to untreated positive symptoms, such as paranoid delusions or hallucinations—"my voices told me to hit people," for example. If substance abuse is thrown into the mix, however, the risk of violence increases dramatically—rising, by one estimate, to 30% of those who have a substance-abuse problem.

derstanding of the nature of mental disorders, and concluded that "the answer appears to be fear of violence . . . the perception of people with psychosis as being dangerous is stronger today than in the past." Every bizarre crime is assumed to be the work of a "madman," a stereotype made stronger by horror movies, whose stock-in-trade is the crazed killer who strikes without warning. Television news and tabloid newspapers with their fixation on "deranged killers" and "homicidal maniacs" help to keep the stereotype alive.

For a parent or sibling of a person newly diagnosed with schizophrenia, it cannot be pleasant to have to cope with the suspicions and stereotypes of friends and neighbors. Some parents report that the best strategy for dealing with the situation is to go public. Barbara, mother of a son with schizophrenia, says it inevitably occurs to parents to try to hide the fact, "but the answer to that is a big NO!! People need to know and you can help by telling them." She recalls that 20 or 30 years ago, "no one talked about schizophrenia. If anything, it was seen as a character flaw. But you know what? Everybody has mental illness somewhere in their family or among their friends."

Frank, father of a son with schizophrenia, agrees with Barbara. "I tell everyone. It started at work. I told about 30 people and I noticed something—about three out of five people say to me that they have a family member with schizophrenia, too, and they're glad to talk about it. Okay, you can see the eyes glaze over in maybe one in ten people that you tell, but just about everybody is okay with it. And I have found that it really helps to get it out in the open."

Parents can help to destroy inaccurate stereotypes by correcting others' faulty assumptions about mental illness.

In addition to being open about their child's illness, parents can help to destroy inaccurate stereotypes by correcting others' faulty assumptions about mental illness. According to Rebecca Woolis, the following are examples of accurate statements that you can make about people with schizophrenia that do not conform to the standard misconceptions about them:

- **All mental illnesses have a strong biological component.** They are not caused by character defects.
- **Schizophrenia affects thinking, behavior, feelings, and judgment.** The person with a mental illness cannot help it.
- **People's functioning fluctuates greatly.** People with mental illness have good days and bad days, just like everyone else.
- **Schizophrenia is not contagious.** People with mental illness do not deserve to be treated the way lepers used to be—segregated and scorned.
- **Mental illness is extremely common.** More than six million Americans have it, and at any given point they occupy more hospital beds than people with cancer, diabetes, arthritis, and heart disease combined.

- The treatment for schizophrenia is limited to symptom reduction and management; there is no cure yet. Cancer, arthritis, heart disease, and diabetes are exactly the same.
- Schizophrenia is a severe disease that may be chronic. The same can be said of diabetes, arthritis, heart disease, and most cancers.

Managing Your Relationship With Your Child: Acceptance and Communication

People with schizophrenia are at great risk of becoming isolated by their illness from normal human relations. As Ian Chovil, a Canadian who has schizophrenia and is a vigorous advocate for patients' inclusion in all aspects of normal life, notes on his website:

> Social isolation has got to be one of the greatest losses in schizophrenia. . . . Although families are usually the main care givers at the beginning of schizophrenia they often find their experience very frustrating for a number of reasons, and relationships suffer. . . . The families tried and tried and lost their ill relative."

In most cases, what destroys relationships among individuals with schizophrenia and their families is the combined effect of a general failure to accept the fact of the illness and anger at the situation, on everybody's part. Psychiatrist E. Fuller Torrey, whose sister has the disease, says that "acceptance puts schizophrenia into perspective as one of life's great tragedies but stops it from becoming a festering sore eating away at life's very core."

An important goal for parents of teenagers who have schizophrenia is maintaining the loving relationship they have had since babyhood. Like many aspects of parenthood, this may be easier said than done: The baby of yesterday is a very different person today, and the parents have experienced a painful, disappointing loss. Nevertheless, the challenge to parents is to find new ways of loving their kids, just as they would if the kids had developed cancer or diabetes. As Rebecca Woolis, an experienced mental health counselor, points out in her handbook, *When Someone You Love Has a Mental Illness:*

> Your love cannot be based solely on who they used to be or on the hope that they will someday be well. They need to feel that you love them today and that you recognize that they are sick today. . . . If you are able to love and accept them as ill, they will more likely be able to accept their illness and limitations.

In addition to accepting the disease and what it has done to their child, parents will need to find a way to address the needs of their sick child without taking away from the needs of their other children and of themselves. The best way to do this is for everyone in the family to learn good communication skills, which will require an understanding of how people with schizophrenia think and learn.

Communicating More Effectively With Your Child: Advice for Parents From Parents

- **Keep it simple.** People with schizophrenia are confused much of the time, not sure what is in their heads versus what is real. Say what you mean, as clearly and directly as you can. "Please wash your hands now, because it's time for dinner," for instance, is preferable to "Go get ready for dinner," which could be confusing or misinterpreted to mean you want the person to cook dinner.
- **Watch for things you say to be taken literally.** People with schizophrenia may misinterpret jokes as insults, for example.

- **Choose your moment to communicate carefully.** If your child is upset, preoccupied with voices or other symptoms, that is no time to bring up a question about something serious, like when he or she is planning to get a job or go back to school.
- **Don't expect clarity from people with schizophrenia, particularly about emotions.** It is always better to pay attention to the emotions they display than to get caught up in their delusional remarks, for example. Frank says that his relationship with his son improved enormously when he stopped arguing about whether his son's ideas were nutty and dealt instead with his anxiety.
- **Don't take your child's delusions personally.** If your child is in a psychotic state and thinks, for example, that you're the devil incarnate, know that this delusional communication is the disease talking, not your child. Try to ignore the delusion and, again, find out what emotion your child is feeling—fear? anxiety?—and talk with him or her about that. You might also ask what would help alleviate this feeling.
- **Don't expect rationality.** If your daughter talks about imaginary visitors in her room at night, there is nothing to be gained by arguing with her. The best thing to say is that while you do not agree with her assessment of the situation, you do understand that the visitors are real to her.
- **Sometimes people with schizophrenia communicate through metaphor.** A young man with the disorder talked from time to time about the Civil War as if it were going on around him, which turned out to be his way of talking about conflicts within his family.
- **Don't be afraid to set rules, but be clear, keep it straightforward, and above all else, be realistic.** People with

schizophrenia are unlikely to stop smoking or drink less coffee because other people want them to, but you can certainly insist that they smoke outdoors and clean up after themselves.

Rebecca Woolis also recommends the following approaches in your communications with your daughter or son:

- Treat her with respect, even if you don't get what she's saying
- Be as supportive and positive as you possibly can
- Try to have casual conversation or share activities with him that you know he is comfortable with
- Never touch her or joke with her unless you know she won't mind
- Don't ask a lot of questions about his private life
- Don't give her advice unless she asks for it
- Avoid touchy topics such as religion, politics, or any other subject that may be involved in his delusional system
- If you don't like some of her behavior, tell her so calmly and specifically

Managing Daily Life

At Home

At some point, it will become clear to families whose members include a person with schizophrenia that living with a seriously disturbed individual can put a huge strain on everyone. Nobody involved in such a situation should underestimate the amount of energy required from each family member just to cope with day-to-day matters. One mother remembers her life as particularly difficult early on in her son's illness: "We would get three or four days of relief when he was in the hospital, but then he would come out and things got bad again. I was terrified, grief-stricken, and had nowhere to go."

That mother's experience was not unique, and it is important for parents to realize that it is not some unique weakness of their own that makes them feel unable to cope with their child's illness: to the contrary, this is a normal reaction. The question is what to do about it. Can you and your family learn to adapt, over time, to the demands of the disorder so that the child can live at home without enormous disruption to one and all in the household? In light of the special challenges of your child's illness, what circumstances in your family can make this adaptation possible or impossible?

It is important for parents to realize that it is not some unique weakness of their own that makes them feel unable to cope with their child's illness.

You and your family will need to take careful stock of your own individual situation and make some very difficult decisions about how well you can accommodate and care for the child who is sick. The first step is to get things out in the open. Nothing is gained and no one feels better by pretending that family life is unchanged by the presence of a member with schizophrenia. The impact of a stressful event such as having to witness one's son or sister in a psychotic state will not be reduced by pretending it didn't happen and avoiding any mention of the obvious. Families can benefit simply from discussing their mutual problems openly, perhaps by having more or less formal family meetings on a regular basis. Sometimes just discussing a problematic situation openly can be enough to reduce the anxiety or worry attached to it. The person with schizophrenia will also benefit from open discussion of the situation, particularly if the meetings lead to clear, sensible guidelines he or she can follow. As one father observed, kids with schizophrenia need and want someone to order the world for them so they can feel in control of themselves. Family rules will be useful in this regard, by setting clear, unambiguous limits on behavior that affects others—no violence, no smoking in bed, no TV or radio after 11 P.M., for example.

Ultimately, though, some families can live with a member who has schizophrenia, and others cannot. There is no right or wrong answer to a highly individual choice that should be made collectively by the parents, the child who has schizophrenia, and any siblings still living at home. Something to avoid at all costs is a setup in which the person with schizophrenia becomes the center of the family, around which all other family members revolve; such a situation is as bad for the sick person as it is for the others. Frank, whose son was diagnosed at 16, has learned to be clear and direct with his son, providing structure through rules and guidelines, but above all by "keeping things simple." On one occasion when his son stopped taking his medication and became psychotic, Frank gave the boy a simple choice: return to intensive daily outpatient therapy or be placed against his will in a locked facility. So far, the results have been satisfactory— the son accepted outpatient therapy, got back on medication, and is doing well.

Obviously, if a patient is flagrantly psychotic, he or she belongs in a locked facility and the decision for the family is a straightforward one. By contrast, a person who has developed a good relationship with a therapy team and knows which medication regimen works best for him is someone who can expect to be able to live more or less independently, just as he would have had he never developed a mental illness. Most of the time, families will fall somewhere in between. The decision of whether to try to live with a relative who has schizophrenia will depend on a number of things, all of which should be discussed openly by the family.

Living With a Person With Schizophrenia: Factors to Consider

It can be done if

- The person with schizophrenia is doing well and has few obvious symptoms.
- The person with schizophrenia has friends and activities he or she is involved with outside the family.
- No siblings live at home who would be negatively affected by being around the person with schizophrenia.
- The family as a whole feels calm, positive, and nonjudgmental toward the person.
- The person with schizophrenia is female.

It is probably not advisable if

- The person's symptoms are so disturbing and disruptive that the rest of the family cannot live a normal life.
- The person has no outside activities or any external support system.
- Siblings live in the home who are negatively affected (e.g., are frightened or feel threatened) by living with the person.
- The family as a whole feels angry, resentful, and critical toward the person.
- The family consists of a single parent, living alone.

Adapted from Rebecca Woolis, *When Someone You Love Has a Mental Illness: A Handbook for Family, Friends, and Caregivers* (pp. 150-151). New York: Jeremy Tarcher/Perigee, 1992.

At School

If you are the parent of a teenager who has developed schizophrenia, it is likely that you will spend a good part of your time dealing with your child's school, be it high school or college. Obviously you will want to secure the best possible placement for your child, who may not be entirely comfortable in a traditional classroom, but while schools are required by law to

It is likely that you will spend a good part of your time dealing with your child's school, be it high school or college.

provide suitable settings for eligible students with disabilities, including mental disorders, they may not readily provide special accommodations for your child without considerable advocacy on your part. As Kate, the mother of a son with schizophrenia and for 20 years a school psychologist, warns: "Negotiating funding for schooling that takes into account a kid's emotional needs will be labor-intensive and not instantly rewarding. Be prepared to have to fight for services at the same time that you're worrying about your kid."

A primary consideration is the extent to which your child's symptoms affect his or her school performance. This will be highly individual—your child may have no problems or many, including

- *Inability to screen out environmental stimuli*—noisy fans during a lecture, for instance, may be misinterpreted by your child as somehow directed to him personally
- *Inability to concentrate*—restlessness, short attention span, and distractibility
- *Difficulty interacting with others*—your child may find it very hard to talk to other students or to participate in class, or she may participate too freely and get laughed at
- *Difficulty handling negative feedback*—your child may overreact to criticism from teachers, and he may prefer to quit school or stop going to class to avoid it
- *Difficulty adjusting to change*—for instance, your child may become very anxious when a scheduled class time is changed

Under federal law, especially the Americans with Disabilities Act (ADA), schools are required to provide "reasonable accommodations" only for those limitations that can be shown to be connected to a student's disability. This means that to get any kind of academic adjustment for their child (e.g., a tutor to help the student with study skills and information retention), parents will have to document those limitations.

PROVING YOUR CHILD'S NEED FOR SERVICES

To determine whether your child needs special accommodations, you should start by talking with a teacher who you think can help you identify the effects of your child's symptoms in the classroom. Kate, however, warns that parents need to be prepared for roadblocks along the way. For example, the teacher may refer your child to the school psychologist for assessment, which may or may not prove worthwhile—many school psychologists have little clinical sophistication and so may miss the crucial symptoms. Or the teacher may dismiss your concerns on the grounds that what you consider to be symptoms are really just signs of normal adolescence. Or your child may be trying to hide her symptoms in the classroom, and the teacher may attribute her classroom performance to stubbornness or inattention. Or if your child is in any way disruptive, says Kate, be prepared for the school to try to "slap the ADHD label on." Among teachers, ADHD, or attention-deficit hyperactivity disorder, is a much-favored explanation of disruptive behavior, in part because the disorder is controllable with medication and is relatively common. Because the symptoms of ADHD—distractibility, impulsivity, attention-demanding behavior—are found in just about everyone at one time or another, it is an easy label to use.

Your child may be trying to hide her symptoms in the classroom, and the teacher may attribute her classroom performance to stubbornness or inattention.

Ultimately, for your child to be considered disabled and therefore eligible for special accommodations, his or her mental illness has to limit one or more of life's "major activities," such as

- Learning
- Thinking
- Concentrating
- Interacting with others
- Caring for oneself
- Speaking
- Performing manual tasks
- Sleeping

In order to prove that your child's functional limitations in school performance are related to his or her mental illness, you will need to get documentation from a licensed mental health professional (psychiatrist, social worker, or clinical psychologist) who has treated your child. The documentation must include diagnosis, specific functional limitations, and an explanation of how they might affect your child in the academic setting and why accommodations are necessary in this case. It must also include the writer's credentials, including license or certification number, area of specialization and expertise, and dates when treatment began and ended. The information must be treated by the school as confidential medical information, with access allowed only to members of the school's disability services office.

REASONABLE ACCOMMODATIONS FOR STUDENTS
WITH MENTAL DISABILITIES

Reasonable accommodations for physically disabled students include such things as wheelchair access and Braille signage. For students with "invisible" mental disabilities, reasonable accommodations will include academic adjustments, such as in the way courses are conducted or academic requirements are met, and the use of auxiliary equipment and personnel. These accommodations will probably have to be negotiated with the school; you as a parent will certainly have to be involved in those negotiations. Here are some examples of reasonable accommodations to look for:

- Classroom accommodations

  - *Preferential seating:* The student should be able to get a seat away from a noisy fan, or one near the door if he or she tends to feel claustrophobic.
  - *Accompanier:* Having someone available to go to class with, and even stay in class with, the student is very reassuring to a person who is anxious or scared.
  - *Beverages permitted in class:* Students on medication are subject to the side effect of dry mouth and should be permitted to have bottled water with them at all times.

- Lecture accommodations

  - *Prearranged breaks:* Students on medication may feel extremely restless and unable to sit still and should be allowed to take short breaks.
  - *Tape recorder:* Students who are anxious about taking notes and afraid of failing might do well to tape-record lectures instead.
  - *Note-taker:* If tape recorders are prohibited, it might help to have someone assigned to take notes for the student.

- Examination accommodations

  - *Change in test format:* It may reduce stress related to examinations if the student is allowed to write an essay rather than to take a multiple-choice test (or vice versa).

- *Extended time:* Having permission to take extra time to complete a test may help the anxious student focus on the test rather than on the clock.
- *Individually proctored exams, even while in the hospital:* It may help an anxious person to take an exam alone, with an individual proctor; such an arrangement could help the student keep up with class even while hospitalized.

- Assignment accommodations

  - *Advance notice of assignments:* It will help the person who gets confused easily to have advance notice of assignments, in writing, so he or she can plan ahead.
  - *Alternative forms of preparation of assigned papers:* The mentally ill student may be better able to demonstrate what he or she has learned in class by writing assignments in a journal, or by speaking them into a tape, rather than by writing a formal essay.
  - *Assignment assistance while in the hospital:* In order to make sure the student keeps up with school work even during a hospitalization, families should stay in touch with the teacher or a disabilities services representative and obtain current assignments for the student to do while in the hospital.

- Administrative accommodations

  - *Flexibility in determining "full-time" status:* For financial aid or insurance purposes, the student may need to be classified as "full time." The school can declare the student as such even if he or she is able to participate in class only on a part-time basis, on the principle that for a person with schizophrenia, a part-time course schedule requires full-time effort.

A Quick-Reference Guide to Helping Your Child in School

To prepare for the possible challenges that their children with schizophrenia may encounter in school, parents should

- Become familiar with the laws that protect people with psychiatric disabilities, such as the ADA.

- Learn how to document the course of their children's disability, that is, to keep a written record of the specific symptoms they have, how many hospitalizations they've had, how long each hospital stay lasted, what medications they've taken, and with what results. Such a record will be invaluable to parents should they need to document problems their children have in school that can be traced directly to their illness. The record will be useful for other things, too, such as summarizing past treatments for any new doctors or therapists that the child may have in the future.

- Learn what are considered "reasonable accommodations" in the classroom for kids with psychiatric disabilities.

- Learn how to file complaints about discrimination in the classroom. For college students, the procedure for filing is outlined at the "Consumer Website for Handling Your Mental Illness at Work and School" (www.bu.edu/cpr/jobschool/), which is sponsored by Boston University's Center for Psychiatric Rehabilitation. For high school students, it will be necessary to contact your local board of education, although you may also find the BU "Consumer Website" helpful as a general guide to the process.

- *Finding a suitable class schedule:* People who take medication or are vulnerable to stress may do better in afternoon classes than in morning ones; choosing a class schedule that best suits a student's needs will make it easier for the student to succeed academically.

- *Incompletes rather than Fs or withdrawal if relapse occurs:* If a student has a relapse of schizophrenia before the end of the semester but has participated up until then, he or she should be entitled to ask for an "incomplete" rather than an F or a withdrawal. An "incomplete" usually means the student will not have to pay to take the course again.

Finding Support for Family and Patient Alike

It will come as no surprise to parents already coping with a child who has schizophrenia that theirs is a very stressful life—even without having to fight with their school system. According to E. Fuller Torrey, a summary of 28 research studies has identified the following problems as common among families that include a member with the disorder:

- No time for friends or social events
- Less money because someone has to be home full-time
- More colds and other minor illnesses among family members

The parents of a person with schizophrenia who lives at home will find themselves having to act as case manager, psychotherapist, nurse, cook, janitor, banker, disciplinarian, and friend—in addition to being a parent and working for a living. This array of roles can be too much for anyone to accomplish successfully, but parents rarely have much choice and must assume some or all of the duties that fall to them.

Even for children with schizophrenia who have moved out on their own, parents will probably continue to play a role in their lives, intervening with landlords, managing their finances, and helping to obtain therapeutic resources. Kate also notes that as parents age, they begin to worry about what will happen to their son or daughter after they die. Additional tasks may include setting up some form of guardianship and financial plan for the child's future.

One of the most important steps that families can take to help themselves along the road of caring for and about an individual with schizophrenia is to get involved in a support group for parents or siblings, where everyone is in the same boat and can offer help and advice along with comfort and encouragement. Kate has learned from experience that no parent can cope alone: "we all need a support group, to laugh, to cry, to share the stress, to not be alone. . . . Everyone there has gone through the same hell." In her experience, family support groups are essential for helping one another learn how to handle the various challenges that may arise: for example, how to call the police, how to handle suicide attempts, and how to fight with hospitals and insurance companies. Christine, another parent, points out that "other parents will answer the questions you don't even know to ask." In fact, every parent interviewed for this book emphatically reiterated the importance of these groups:

> *Get involved in a support group for parents or siblings, where everyone is in the same boat and can offer help and advice along with comfort and encouragement.*

- "Get connected! Do it even if you've been taking care of a child with schizophrenia for 20 years! Even after 20 years, you may not know everything that's available to help you."
- "Get into a support group or a network like NAMI. Finding quality care is HARD, especially if you don't have a lot of money. You will need peer support."
- "Support groups help you cope. It doesn't matter if they're organized groups or informal ones; you need to know you're not alone."

- "Get into family support EARLY! It's lifesaving."
- "Support groups will help you get over feeling embarrassed. You'll get knowledge, support, and understanding."

Organizations that can put families in touch with support groups in their area include NAMI and the National Mental Health Association. There are also organizations that can provide support to patients themselves, including Schizophrenics Anonymous, Recovery, Inc., and the National Mental Health Consumers' Self-Help Clearinghouse. Complete contact information for these organizations is provided in the Resources section of this book.

Paul: A Story of Recovery

In 1994, on October 15—a date he remembers because it was on the identification band placed on his wrist at the hospital—Paul ceased to be a sophomore studying engineering at a major university, with plans to go on to medical school. Instead, he became a psychiatric patient. This came about when he suddenly believed that someone he knew was a recruiter for the CIA who had determined that Paul should join their ranks. Terrified, Paul went to the university chapel to hide, but his frantic behavior attracted the attention of the campus police, who arrested him and took him to the nearest hospital. Two weeks later, he was discharged, not to return to school, but back home, to his parents' care.

Paul had been a good student in high school, and he and his family had great hopes for him. He found college very difficult, however, both socially and academically. After one year, his grades were poor enough that he lost his scholarship—"my only ticket to financial independence." He kept this devastating news to himself over the summer while working as a camp counselor, and returned to school determined to get the scholarship back so he could continue his studies. In retrospect, Paul has decided that his psychotic break in October 1994 was the direct result of his being told by the dean of the engineering school that there was no hope for a scholarship and that he would not be able to resume his studies. He was particularly distraught by the realization that he would have to tell his parents—a nurse and a cab driver, both of whom had always been deeply proud of his academic accomplishments—that he was all washed up as a student at the age of 18.

The next few years were spent working at temporary jobs, except for the weeks here and there when he was rehospitalized. Early on, he briefly attended a day program, which he didn't like—"It was totally boring, really Mickey Mouse stuff; we baked cookies and learned how to read maps"—but for a while his therapy was conducted on an outpatient basis, except when he went back to the hospital. Each hospitalization was precipitated by the same thing: Paul stopped taking his medication, sometimes because he couldn't handle a particular drug, and other times because the drugs he was on weren't working effectively. But mostly he stopped his medication "because I was in denial. Denial is the first thing you'll come up against if you get sick, because there's no X-ray or CAT scan that can tell you you're sick, so you have trouble believing that you really are. I guess we just have to keep proving it to ourselves."

Paul learned that no matter what else happens, he must take his medicine. "I finally learned: If I take it, I'm

> "Denial is the first thing you'll come up against if you get sick, because there's no X-ray or CAT scan that can tell you you're sick, so you have trouble believing that you really are."

just as normal as anyone else." Nevertheless, this knowledge was acquired the hard way, over almost a decade: "For a while there, I was hospitalized at least once a year." Two persistent problems interfered in his attempts at recovery: his denial of being ill and the fact that he found it difficult to function on the job because his medications made him sleepy. "I had this one job I liked, but I couldn't always do it because my meds made me so tired that one day I fell asleep in the food court, and when I woke up, I knew I'd be fired. I remember I sat in that food court and cried."

Paul believes that the program that really enabled him to turn the corner into recovery was a transitional housing program sponsored by the academic medical center where he has gotten all his previous treatment, from hospitalizations to out-patient visits. The program incorporated a day program and housing—"well, let's face it, it's really a homeless shelter, but it's a nice homeless shelter." The staff there "really cared about me—I had the best room, with only one roommate, who was a very nice guy, and it was air conditioned, and that worked out well."

Paul's success at the transitional housing program, which caters to young adults with mental illness who become home-less, enabled him to "graduate," as he put it, into a young adult housing program funded by his city's department of mental health. Paul describes this as

> a phenomenal program called a supervised apartment, where three of us lived in a nice apartment with spacious rooms and porches and we each had our own bedroom, and the staff checked on us every few days or so to make sure we were doing all right. We had these competitive dinner parties with other apartments, to see who could put on the best dinner, and we took trips and we even went on a vacation to Maine together one summer. My roommate was a good

influence on me, too: He's not brilliant but he never gives up and has an awesome work ethic; and for the first time since 1994 I did not have my annual hospitalization the whole time I was in the apartment program. The minute I got there, I decided God was watching over me.

Today, Paul lives in his own apartment and works full time as an advocate for mentally ill teenagers and young adults. Acting as co-chair of a committee formed to oversee the outcome of various programs from the point of view of consumers (patients), he has worked on research projects analyzing the effectiveness of housing programs like the ones he lived in himself. In his current job, he writes grants and is proud of having testified formally at state-wide meetings of the mental health department, not once but twice, acting as advocate and consumer. He continues in treatment with his psychiatrist, takes his meds, and admits that "sometimes the stress of doing this public stuff gets to me." Not long ago, Paul was briefly rehospitalized, which he is "a bit embarrassed about; I guess you could say I went in for a tune-up. I still have problems getting to work— I have to push myself—and I don't think I work up to my own expectations."

Paul believes in looking on the bright side of things, though. "I got that from one of my psychiatrists, because he always said, 'Paul, things will get better.' And you know what? They really did." He credits two things for his recovery: his family and his doctors. "My doctors are the best; they really care. One of them even visited me in the hospital after he wasn't my doctor any more, and another one took the time to answer ALL my mom's questions about my illness, no matter how long it took. Having a doctor willing to communicate with my parents was especially important, because any doctor who deals with young persons needs to talk with parents who are scared and frustrated, especially if [their kids] are over 18—the parents still need to know."

As for his family, Paul says:

They're really the best. I have the best mom, the best dad, and the best siblings. They never gave up on me, but they don't let me get away with stuff, either. But you know, I have to admit that it was my [supervised apartment] program that was the key to my recovery. What you have to remember is that mental illness is even bigger than your family, that a lot of recovery means doing stuff for yourself. My family was great because my parents acted like birds, who feed their babies and teach them to fly, pushing them out of the nest when they're ready to be on their own. My dad, for example, wants me to have the opportunity to recover and take care of myself, so he never let me quit my programs. So you see, my doctor was right: things can get better.

Chapter Five

Prevention of Schizophrenia: The Challenges

W ith the advent of newer, "atypical" antipsychotic medi-
cines, we have seen that the principal symptoms of
schizophrenia can usually be controlled. We are not yet able to
address some of the behavioral aspects of the disorder as efficiently, however. The general failure of traditional outpatient
therapy programs to address the social and vocational needs of
people with schizophrenia has led to the development of intensive, individualized treatment initiatives, such as Assertive
Community Treatment (ACT), designed to restore patients to
genuine participation in all aspects of adult life. But no matter
how successful programs are at reintegrating people with schizophrenia into society, most people would agree that it would be
even better if we could prevent them from becoming sick in
the first place.

There are two steps in prevention of any disease: identification of who is at risk, and successful treatment of those identified. As a general rule, prevention of disease is achieved at three
levels. Primary prevention is practiced prior to the onset of
the disease in question, as with vaccination; secondary prevention refers to interventions made after the disease has been

recognized but before it has caused suffering and disability; and tertiary prevention is employed subsequent to the onset of suffering or disability, to prevent further deterioration. In the case of schizophrenia, early detection and prevention of the illness are not yet entirely possible, because there are no universal signs of the disorder; moreover, the disease itself is not yet fully understood. In hopes of being able to intervene preventively, some researchers are currently working to identify a full range of risk factors for schizophrenia, while others are focusing on identifying signal events that occur prior to the onset of the disease.

Some researchers are currently working to identify a full range of risk factors for schizophrenia, while others are focusing on identifying signal events that occur prior to the onset of the disease.

As a general rule, schizophrenia does not develop all of a sudden. Some studies have identified signs of future schizophrenia in children as early as infancy, noting that some babies whose ability to form social relationships was limited were at risk for developing schizophrenia in later years. Other studies noted that children at risk for schizophrenia had less social contact with their mothers and less fear of strangers than normal, in addition to being temperamental and difficult in general. A preference for solitary play combined with poor social confidence in childhood and early adolescence are associated with later schizophrenia, as is impulsiveness and emotional instability. Poor relationships with other children in general are the characteristics most often predictive of later schizophrenia.

Families themselves are often able to describe vague, ill-defined symptoms occurring weeks, months, or even years before their relatives developed schizophrenia, strongly suggesting the existence of a preliminary stage of disease. Looking back, most parents can probably identify some changes that took place in their children before the disease process was established and symptoms emerged. Some examples are depressed moods, changes in behavior, reduced ability to function socially and in school, vaguely psychotic ideas, and other nonspecific signs that something is not right, all of which can and may occur long before the first psychotic episode takes place. And in retrospect, some parents of individuals with schizophrenia realize that some or even all of their children's early developmental milestones— that is, sitting, standing, walking, and talking—were slightly delayed, but not to such an extent that they had been alarmed by the delay at the time.

The period before any disease is fully developed is called the *prodrome* (see Chapter 2, p. 13, for a list of prodromal and other early symptoms of schizophrenia), and it is hoped that eventually it will be possible to intervene early during this time to prevent the onset of psychosis or to improve its outcome by delaying or preventing the process in which negative symptoms develop and lead to the kind of deterioration associated with chronic schizophrenia in adults. It is the hope of researchers that by identifying children at risk early, and by intervening promptly, the development of long-range symptoms might be avoided altogether. For instance, if researchers can identify the neurological and cognitive precursors to schizophrenia before the disease manifests itself, it might be possible to develop new somatic therapies that target the dysfunctional neural networks involved.

The value of such preventive measures lies in the hope that early intervention in the disease process might derail the gradual deterioration seen in people with schizophrenia who have experienced many relapses into psychosis, from which they recover less and less fully over time. Therapies available today can only partially forestall the degenerative process that is characteristic of the disease, which makes the prospect of prevention all the more desirable.

Although psychiatry has learned a great deal about schizophrenia in the past few years, several areas of research must remain a priority:

- Identification of reliable early signs of disease in people at high risk for psychosis
- Identification of the beginning of the psychotic process for the purpose of intervening early
- Identification of signs and symptoms of the first psychotic episode that can predict subsequent illness course
- Identification of the role played by early neurodevelopment in the psychotic process
- Specialized studies of adolescent-onset schizophrenia, as opposed to more generalized studies of the disorder
- Education of the public and health care workers in the early signs and symptoms of schizophrenia to promote early intervention

If more people knew that the symptoms of schizophrenia that seem so scary are just that—symptoms of a disease—they might be less unnerved by them.

Until such time as we know enough about schizophrenia to be able to prevent its occurrence, the best we can hope for is swift intervention based on early detection of prodromal signs or symptoms that are precursors to the illness. Parents can play a role in this regard. Because they are in the best position to see and describe early, prodromal signs of developing schizophrenia in adolescent children, it is particularly important that they be aware of the early symptoms and able to recognize them. In many communities, schizophrenia is poorly understood, and people may fear it for all the wrong reasons. If more people knew that the symptoms of schizophrenia that seem so scary are just that—symptoms of a disease—they might be less unnerved by them.

Barbara, the mother of a son with schizophrenia and a long-time activist, believes that schools can and should play a central role in any effort to educate parents and teachers about schizophrenia and the importance of early intervention:

> The schools are the only social institution in this country that is truly universal—every town has schools and everybody goes to school at some time or other—so it is absolutely essential to get handouts, brochures, booklets, whatever, into the schools. Information about schizophrenia—what it is, who is at risk, what its symptoms are, what to look for, and where to go when you find it! That's what we have to get into the schools, so parents and teachers know what to look for. Then the schools should know how to refer parents to organizations like NAMI. That's the way to get kids in for early intervention.

Chapter Six

Conclusion: A Call for Action

Families . . . are already burdened enough by having a family member with a psychiatric condition. What we need are systems that help the families. We need lots of one-on-one help for families and for people with psychiatric conditions. We need an army of foot soldiers—consumers helping patients, consumers calling other consumers, outreach workers—anything that cuts the isolation, the stigma, the fear, and the burden.

—Moe Armstrong, psychiatric consumer and advocate

In 1979 the National Alliance on Mental Illness (NAMI) was founded by parents of children with serious mental illnesses, including schizophrenia. The founding members were brought together by a shared need for emotional support and for information about coping strategies and resources that they could draw on to confront the devastating impact of severe mental illness on their families. Out of their early meetings, however, came the realization that there is power in numbers, and the members of NAMI figured out that collectively they were in a good position to exert political pressure on their state governments to develop adequate services for the mentally ill. Today, NAMI is a nonprofit, grassroots, self-help, support and advocacy organization of patients (consumers), families, and friends of people with severe mental illnesses who work, according to NAMI's website,

> to achieve equitable services and treatment for more than 15 million Americans living with severe mental illnesses and their families. Hundreds of thousands of volunteers participate in more than one thousand local affiliates and fifty state organizations to provide education and support, combat stigma, support increased funding for research, and advocate for adequate health insurance, housing, rehabilitation, and jobs for people with mental illnesses and their families.

NAMI is now an enormous national organization that lobbies on behalf of its members, and any parent of a child with a serious mental illness such as schizophrenia should join it, whether for support, to become active, or both.

Obtaining Essential Services

Among the problems facing parents of children with schizophrenia is the perpetual lack of useful services. While it is relatively easy to find medical personnel able to prescribe antipsychotic medication, it is by no means easy to find anything else—outpatient programs, day treatment facilities, housing, social or vocational rehabilitation programs, educational support, or clinics willing to work with people who have schizophrenia. Parents can work through NAMI to expand the range of services available to adolescents and young adults with schizophrenia.

The loosely connected organizations, institutions, and programs that make up what is known as the mental health system

Among the problems facing parents of children with schizophrenia is the perpetual lack of useful services.

in this country are constantly beset with problems of funding, particularly when it comes to serious and persistent diseases like schizophrenia. So entrenched is the opposition to providing many of the vital services needed by seriously mentally ill patients that in 1999 the surgeon general of the United States introduced his Report on Mental Illness with the observation that in spite of all the progress made in neuroscientific research into brain diseases of all sorts, barriers to their treatment continued to persist throughout the country. While some of the barriers are social and discriminatory, others are purely financial and involve the refusal of insurance companies to reimburse for certain services. As the surgeon general put it, "We have allowed stigma and a now unwarranted sense of hopelessness about the opportunities for recovery from mental illness to erect these barriers."

Yet the barriers persist. Parents interviewed for this book took it for granted that newly diagnosed patients would be turned away from outpatient programs that prefer to treat the "worried well." Social and vocational rehabilitation programs, if they exist at all, are considered "clubs" by insurance companies, who will not pay for their services. For its part, Medicaid, which pays for about half of all public mental health services, considers all mental health services to be optional; individual states are not required to cover them. Assertive Community Treatment (ACT) programs promise intensive, individualized treatment plans with flexible implementation tailor-made for each patient, but so far they only exist in some states, though there are rumors of more to come. Medicaid considers ACT treatment optional, and few states have opted to include the service among the therapies they are willing to fund. Psychiatric consumers—former patients—develop thoughtful approaches to making the daily lives of other consumers more normal and less focused on their illness, but their programs are tiny, localized, and dependent on the charismatic leadership of their founders; moreover, they have yet to be replicated.

At this time, it seems to be the case that unless they are rich, all that people with schizophrenia can count on in the way of therapy is to be treated symptomatically with medication, with intermittent brief stays in hospitals if they relapse. Little is available to help them and their families adjust to life with a chronic disease that interferes in social and vocational function. Working through NAMI to demand the restoration of fully funded rehabilitation services for the seriously mentally ill is something parents can and should consider doing. Indeed, through NAMI or another national advocacy organization, parents can become politically active, lobbying for services that go beyond medication for symptom control to help people with schizophrenia achieve recovery. Supported employment and supported education programs like the ones described in Chapter 3—Jump Start, The Village, and the Michigan Supported Education Program are good examples—are an endangered species and in notoriously short supply, even though evidence has been collected that shows they are effective, and parents whose children could benefit from them should demand that their state offices of mental health sponsor more of them. Programs like WestBridge that tackle both schizophrenia and substance abuse together are also in very short supply, even though it is well known that young people with schizophrenia are extremely likely to experiment with various substances. Working nationally and within their own states, parents can and should demand badly needed recovery-oriented programs that recognize the fact that people with serious mental illness are capable of living lives of hope rather than despair.

Educating Others

Every parent of a child or adolescent with schizophrenia is in a good position to educate others about the disease. As Frank and Barbara have both said, go public with your personal story. Not only will you feel better by doing so, but you will help others realize that it is a good idea to speak out. Frank found that three out of every five people with whom he spoke openly about his son's diagnosis revealed that they, too, had relatives who were seriously mentally ill. Presumably Frank's openness also helped the two out of five who didn't have mentally ill relatives, by teaching them something they hadn't known before, which is that some people are not ashamed of acknowledging this dimension of the human condition. Parents who speak up to their friends and colleagues about the diseases afflicting their children are striking the most effective possible blow against stigma by showing others that not everyone is embarrassed, ashamed, or afraid of the mentally ill.

Glossary

5-HTT   A gene that helps regulate the amount of serotonin in the brain. A variant of the gene that produces low levels of serotonin has been linked to certain anxiety disorders.

accommodation   A change that helps a person overcome or work around a disability.

acute post-traumatic stress disorder   Post-traumatic stress disorder that lasts from one to three months.

acute stress disorder   An anxiety disorder that develops following exposure to a traumatic event and lasts no more than one month. It is characterized by reexperiencing the trauma, avoidance, increased arousal, and dissociative symptoms.

adrenal glands   Glands located just above the kidneys. Their hormones help regulate many physiological functions, including the body's stress response.

adrenocorticotropic hormone (ACTH)   A hormone released by the pituitary gland.

agoraphobia   Avoidance associated with panic disorder. It is characterized by fear and associated avoidance of places or situations from which escape might be difficult or help might not be available in the event of a panic attack.

amygdala   A structure inside the brain that plays a central role in the fear response.

anorexia nervosa   An eating disorder in which people have an intense fear of becoming fat, leading them to severely restrict what they eat, often to the point of near starvation.

antidepressant   A medication used to prevent or relieve depression.

anxiety   The apprehensive anticipation of future danger or misfortune.

anxiety disorder   Any of a group of disorders characterized by excessive fear or worry that is recurrent or long-lasting. The symptoms of the disorder cause distress or interfere with day-to-day activities.

attention-deficit hyperactivity disorder (ADHD)   A disorder characterized by a short attention span, excessive activity, or impulsive behavior.

atypical antipsychotic   One of the newer antipsychotic medications. Some atypical antipsychotics are also used as mood stabilizers.

autonomic nervous system   The portion of the nervous system that controls involuntary functions of internal organs.

axon   The sending branch on a nerve cell.

basal ganglia   A cluster of neurons within the brain that plays a key role in movement and behavior.

behavioral inhibition   A type of temperament in which individuals are typically irritable as infants, fearful as toddlers, and shy and wary as school-aged children.

benzodiazepine   An antianxiety medication that is thought to raise levels of gamma-amino-butyric acid in the brain.

beta-blocker   A medication that is usually prescribed for high blood pressure or heart problems. Beta-blockers are also occasionally prescribed for performance anxiety.

body dysmorphic disorder   An obsessive-compulsive spectrum disorder in which people become so preoccupied with an imagined defect in their appearance that it causes serious distress or significant problems in their everyday life.

bulimia nervosa   An eating disorder in which people binge on large quantities of food, then purge by forced vomiting, laxative or diuretic abuse, or excessive exercise.

buspirone (BuSpar)   An antianxiety medication that increases serotonin activity in the brain while decreasing dopamine activity.

cerebral cortex   The part of the brain that is responsible for higher-order thought processes, such as language and information processing.

chronic post-traumatic stress disorder   Post-traumatic stress disorder that lasts longer than three months.

classical conditioning   A mental association that is formed by pairing a previously neutral stimulus with a stimulus that produces an innate response. Over time, the previously neutral stimulus becomes able to bring on the response by itself.

cognitive-behavioral therapy (CBT)   A form of therapy that helps people recognize and change self-defeating thought patterns as well as identify and change maladaptive behaviors.

comorbidity   The coexistence of two or more disorders in the same individual.

compulsion   A repetitive behavioral or mental act that a person feels driven to perform in response to an obsession or according to rigid rules.

conduct disorder   A disorder characterized by a repetitive or persistent pattern of having extreme difficulty following rules or conforming to social norms.

corticotropin-releasing factor (CRF)   A hormone released by the hypothalamus.

cortisol   A hormone released by the adrenal glands that is responsible for many of the physiological effects of stress.

depression A disorder that involves either being in a low mood or irritable nearly all the time, or losing interest or enjoyment in almost everything.

***Diagnostic and Statistical Manual of Mental Disorders*, Fourth Edition, Text Revision (*DSM-IV-TR*)** A manual that mental health professionals use for diagnosing mental disorders.

disruptive behavior disorder A disorder that leads to very troublesome behavior; for example, attention-deficit hyperactivity disorder, conduct disorder, or oppositional defiant disorder.

domestic violence Violence that occurs within the context of an intimate relationship, such as marriage or dating.

dopamine A neurotransmitter that is essential for movement and also influences motivation and perception of reality.

eating disorder A disorder characterized by serious disturbances in eating behavior. People may severely restrict what they eat, or they may go on eating binges, then attempt to compensate by such means as self-induced vomiting or misuse of laxatives.

emotional processing theory A theory of anxiety disorders in which fear is defined as a cognitive structure that serves as a blueprint for escaping or avoiding danger. Different anxiety disorders reflect different structures.

exposure and response prevention (EX/RP) A form of cognitive-behavioral therapy that is used to treat obsessive-compulsive disorder. The exposure part involves having people confront the thoughts or situations that provoke their obsessional distress, while the response prevention part means voluntarily refraining from using compulsions to reduce their distress during these encounters.

exposure and ritual prevention See exposure and response prevention.

exposure therapy A form of cognitive-behavioral therapy in which people are taught to systematically confront a feared object or situation under safe conditions. The goal is to allow them to learn that the feared stimuli are not actually dangerous.

extinction The weakening of a response that has been learned through classical conditioning.

eye movement desensitization and reprocessing (EMDR) A form of therapy for post-traumatic stress disorder that combines elements of exposure therapy with directed shifts in attention.

gamma-amino-butyric acid (GABA) A neurotransmitter that inhibits the flow of nerve signals in neurons by blocking the release of other neurotransmitters. It is thought to help quell anxiety.

generalized anxiety disorder (GAD) An anxiety disorder characterized by excessive anxiety and worry over a number of different things.

generalized social anxiety disorder Social anxiety disorder that occurs in most social situations.

group therapy   Therapy that brings together a group of people with similar emotional or behavioral problems, who meet with a therapist to work on specific treatment goals.

health maintenance organization (HMO)   A type of managed care plan in which members must use health care providers who work for the HMO.

hippocampus   A brain structure involved in emotion, learning, and memory.

hypochondriasis   An obsessive-compulsive spectrum disorder in which people become preoccupied with the idea that they have a serious illness, based on their misinterpretation of harmless bodily signs and sensations.

hypothalamic-pituitary-adrenal (HPA) axis   A body system comprising the hypothalamus, pituitary gland, and adrenal glands along with the substances these structures secrete.

hypothalamus   Part of the brain that serves as the command center for the nervous and hormonal systems.

individualized educational plan (IEP)   A written educational plan for an individual student who qualifies for services under IDEA.

Individuals with Disabilities Education Improvement Act of 2004 (IDEA)   The federal special education law, which applies to students who have a disability that impacts their ability to benefit from general educational services.

insomnia   Difficulty falling or staying asleep.

irritable bowel syndrome   A stress-related digestive disorder in which the large intestine doesn't function properly, leading to symptoms such as abdominal cramps, bloating, constipation, or diarrhea.

learning disorder   A disorder that adversely affects a person's performance in school or ability to function in everyday situations that require reading, writing, or math skills.

least restrictive environment   The setting that allows a student with a disability to be educated alongside peers without disabilities to the greatest extent possible while still meeting his or her individual needs.

managed care   A system designed to control health care costs.

Medicaid   A public insurance program, paid for by a combination of federal and state funds, that provides health and mental health care to low-income individuals who meet eligibility criteria.

medical necessity   A standard used by managed care plans in determining whether or not to pay for a health care service. To satisfy this standard, the service must be deemed medically appropriate and necessary to meet a patient's health care needs.

mental health parity   A policy that attempts to equalize the way that mental and physical illnesses are covered by health plans.

mood stabilizer   A medication that helps even out extreme mood swings.

neuron   A cell in the brain or another part of the nervous system that is specialized to send, receive, and process information.

neurotransmitter   A chemical that acts as a messenger within the brain.

norepinephrine   A neurotransmitter that helps regulate arousal, sleep, and blood pressure. Excessive amounts of norepinephrine may trigger anxiety.

obsession   A recurrent thought, impulse, or mental image that is perceived as intrusive and inappropriate, and that provokes anxiety and distress.

obsessive-compulsive disorder (OCD)   An anxiety disorder characterized by recurrent, uncontrollable obsessions or compulsions.

obsessive-compulsive spectrum disorder   Any of a group of disorders that resemble obsessions or compulsions and may respond to some of the same treatments as obsessive-compulsive disorder.

oppositional defiant disorder   A disorder characterized by a persistent pattern of unusually frequent defiance, hostility, or lack of cooperation.

panic attack   A sudden, unexpected wave of intense fear and apprehension that is accompanied by physical symptoms, such as a rapid heart rate, shortness of breath, or sweating.

panic disorder   An anxiety disorder characterized by the repeated occurrence and fear of spontaneous panic attacks. The fear results from the belief that such attacks will result in catastrophes, such as having a heart attack.

pediatric autoimmune neuropsychiatric disorders associated with streptococcal infections (PANDAS)   An uncommon childhood form of obsessive-compulsive disorder that is brought on by a strep infection.

performance anxiety   A limited form of social anxiety in which the excessive fear relates to performing a specific task in front of others.

pituitary gland   A small gland located at the base of the brain. Its hormones control other glands and help regulate growth, metabolism, and reproduction.

placebo   A sugar pill that looks like a real medication, but does not contain an active ingredient.

point of service (POS) plan   A type of managed care plan that is similar to a traditional health maintenance organization (HMO) or preferred provider organization (PPO), except that members can also use providers outside the HMO organization or PPO network in exchange for a higher copayment or deductible.

post-traumatic stress disorder (PTSD)   An anxiety disorder that develops following exposure to a traumatic event. Symptoms include reexperiencing the trauma, avoidance and emotional numbing, and increased arousal.

preferred provider organization (PPO)   A type of managed care plan in which members may choose from a network of providers who have contracts with the PPO.

prefrontal cortex   The front part of the cerebral cortex. It is involved in complex thought, problem solving, and emotion.

protective factor   A characteristic that decreases a person's likelihood of developing a disorder.

psychiatrist   A medical doctor who specializes in the diagnosis and treatment of mental illnesses and emotional problems.

psychological debriefing A mental health service that is provided to survivors immediately after a traumatic event. The goal is to help survivors understand their feelings, reduce their distress, and prepare for what they may face in the future.

psychologist (clinical) A mental health professional who provides assessment and therapy for mental and emotional disorders.

randomized controlled trial A study in which participants are randomly assigned to a treatment group or a control group. The control group typically receives either a placebo, a nonspecific psychotherapy, or standard care. This study design allows researchers to determine which changes in the treatment group over time are due to the treatment itself.

receptor A molecule that recognizes a specific chemical, such as a neurotransmitter. For a chemical message to be sent from one nerve cell to another, the message must be delivered to a matching receptor on the surface of the receiving nerve cell.

reuptake The process by which a neurotransmitter is absorbed back into the sending branch of the nerve cell that originally released it.

risk factor A characteristic that increases a person's likelihood of developing a disorder.

school refusal Extreme reluctance to go to school.

Section 504 A section of the Rehabilitation Act of 1973 that applies to students who have a physical and mental impairment that substantially limits one or more major life activity.

selective mutism An uncommon disorder in which children who are physically and mentally capable of speaking completely refuse to talk in certain social situations.

selective serotonin reuptake inhibitor (SSRI) An antidepressant that affects the concentration and activity of serotonin in the brain. SSRIs are widely prescribed for anxiety disorders as well as depression.

separation anxiety disorder An anxiety disorder, found mainly in children, that involves excessive anxiety about being separated from the parent or home.

serotonin A neurotransmitter that helps regulate mood, sleep, appetite, and sexual drive. Low levels of serotonin have been linked to both anxiety and depression.

serotonin–norepinephrine reuptake inhibitor (SNRI) An antidepressant that affects the concentration and activity of serotonin and norepinephrine in the brain. SNRIs are prescribed for anxiety disorders as well as depression.

side effect An unintended effect of a drug.

social anxiety disorder An anxiety disorder characterized by marked fear in social situations where the person is exposed to unfamiliar people or possible scrutiny by others.

social phobia See social anxiety disorder.

specific phobia An anxiety disorder characterized by an intense fear that is focused on a specific animal, object, activity, or situation, and that is out of proportion to any real threat.

stigma Stereotyping, prejudice, and discrimination that are directed toward a particular group of people.

strep throat An infection of the throat caused by streptococcus bacteria. It is characterized by a sore throat, fever, and swollen lymph nodes in the neck.

substance abuse The continued use of alcohol or other drugs despite negative consequences, such as dangerous behavior while under the influence or substance-related personal, social, or legal problems.

support group A group of people with a common problem who get together to share emotional support, practical advice, and sometimes educational resources.

synapse The gap that separates nerve cells.

temperament A person's inborn tendency to react to events in a particular way, which remains relatively stable over time.

thalamus A brain structure that acts as a relay station for incoming sensory information.

tic A sudden, rapid, repetitive movement or vocalization.

Tourette's syndrome A neurological disorder characterized by frequent, multiple tics.

transporter A molecule that carries a chemical messenger, called a neurotransmitter, back to the nerve cell that originally sent the message.

trichotillomania An obsessive-compulsive spectrum disorder in which people feel driven to pull out their own hair, leading to noticeable hair loss.

tricyclic antidepressant An older class of antidepressant that affects the concentration and activity of serotonin and norepinephrine in the brain. Tricyclic antidepressants are prescribed for anxiety disorders as well as depression.

Resources

Essential Reading
All of the books (and websites) included in this list were recommended by at least one of the parents who were interviewed for this book.

Chovil, Ian. The Experience of Schizophrenia. www.chovil.com.
This website is maintained by a Canadian man who has schizophrenia. Mr. Chovil is very frank and open in describing his own problems with his disease, his family, and his social isolation. This would be a good website to forward to teenagers who have just been diagnosed with the disease.

Deveson, Anne. *Tell Me I'm Here: One Family's Experience of Schizophrenia*. New York: Penguin Books, 1991.
This book is written by a journalist, an Australian documentary filmmaker, whose son developed schizophrenia in his teens. The book is engaging and very candid about what it was like to live with a young man who rarely complied with his treatment regimen and who wound up addicted to illegal drugs, eking out a marginal existence within a hippie-like subculture. His mother tried very hard to avert that outcome and is honest about her inability—and that of the Australian mental health system—to help her son.

Neugeboren, Jay. *Transforming Madness: New Lives for People Living with Mental Illness*. New York: William Morrow and Company, 1999.
Mr. Neugeboren is the designated caretaker of his brother, who has schizophrenia. In this book, he writes of the efforts of a few dedicated ex-patients who have overcome schizophrenia well enough to be able to work, get married, and have children. Many of them have become activists and seek now to develop effective programs for the rehabilitation of others.

Torrey, E. Fuller. *Surviving Schizophrenia: A Manual for Families, Consumers, and Providers.* Fourth edition. New York: Quill, 2001.
This book provides a wealth of information and was written by a well-known psychiatrist whose sister has schizophrenia. Some parents interviewed noted that the book is organized in a confusing way, and several felt it was too long.

Wechsler, James A. *In a Darkness.* New York: Irvington Publishers, 1983.
Even though this is a relatively old book that may be hard to find, it is worth looking for. The author was a journalist whose son developed schizophrenia while in his freshman year in college, and the book details the intense efforts the author, his wife, and daughter made in their effort to obtain effective treatment for their son and brother. The book is beautifully written and describes very painful events and failures from a parent's point of view.

Woolis, Rebecca. *When Someone You Love Has a Mental Illness: A Handbook for Family, Friends, and Caregivers.* New York: Jeremy Tarcher/Perigee, 1992.
Every one of the parents interviewed for this book recommended Woolis's book as the one they had personally found most helpful. One mother described the book as "tactful, gentle, and practical."

Organizations and Services

American Academy of Child and Adolescent Psychiatry
3615 Wisconsin Avenue N.W.
Washington, DC 20016-3007
(202) 966-7300
www.aacap.org

American Academy of Pediatrics
141 Northwest Point Boulevard
Elk Grove Village, IL 60007-1098
(847) 434-4000
www.aap.org

American Association of Suicidology
4201 Connecticut Avenue N.W., Suite 408
Washington, DC 20008
(202) 237-2280
www.suicidology.org

American Foundation for Suicide Prevention
120 Wall Street, 22nd Floor
New York, NY 10005
(888) 333-2377
www.afsp.org

American Psychiatric Association
1000 Wilson Boulevard, Suite 1825
Arlington, VA 22209-3901
(703) 907-7300
www.psych.org

American Psychological Association
750 First Street N.E.
Washington, DC 20002-4242
(800) 374-2721
www.apa.org

Bazelon Center for Mental Health Law
1101 15th Street N.W., Suite 1212
Washington, DC 20005
(202) 467-5730
www.bazelon.org

> Named for a federal court judge whose decisions permitted thousands of long-time institutionalized people to be discharged from custodial institutions, the Bazelon Center for Mental Health Law is an activist organization dedicated to patients' rights. Their website provides links to lists of lawyers who specialize in mental health law.

Boston University Center for Psychiatric Rehabilitation
940 Commonwealth Avenue West
Boston, MA 02215
www.bu.edu/cpr

> The Center's "Consumer website for Handling Your Mental Illness at Work and School" can be accessed at www.bu.edu/cpr/jobschool/
>
> This organization is affiliated with Sargent College of Health and Rehabilitation Sciences and the Department of Rehabilitation Counseling at Boston University, which has sponsored some innovative work in the field of psychosocial rehabilitation. The center is interested in research, training, and service provision, and they are "dedicated to improving the lives of persons who have psychiatric disabilities by improving the effectiveness of people, programs, and service systems." Their website is an important resource for any parent who is trying to obtain academic adjustments for a child or adolescent with schizophrenia.

Gould Farm
P.O. Box 157
Monterey, MA 01245
(413) 528-1804
www.gouldfarm.org

> Founded in 1900, Gould Farm is the oldest therapeutic community in the United States. It describes its services as follows:

The Gould Farm Communities (hereafter referred to as Gould Farm) comprise a psychosocial rehabilitation program that is steeped in the tradition of social service and fellowship. A compassionate, respectful family environment where people with mental illness learn to build more meaningful lives for themselves, Gould Farm provides many opportunities for "guests" to address individual goals. Many people with psychiatric disabilities struggle in frustration on the margins of society. Gould Farm invites them into the heart of its communities. Our services remain rooted in the belief that every person has something valuable to contribute to the community regardless of their mental or emotional limitations, and we assist in developing the strengths to realize these gifts as they proceed on their road to independence.

The Gould Farm is a private, nonprofit facility that accepts no government funding of any kind, but assures visitors to its website that any family willing to make full financial disclosure will be considered for financial aid, as is the case for 40% of its "guests."

Institute for Recovery and Community Integration
1211 Chestnut Street
12th Floor
Philadelphia, PA 19107
(215) 751-1800 (ext. 265)
www.mhasp.org/mhrecovery/index.html

The Institute for Recovery and Community Integration states its mission as follows:

> to introduce and advance the principles of mental health recovery, peer support and community integration as the catalyst for transforming individual lives and also local, state, and national mental health systems. The Institute seeks to establish personal empowerment, attitudinal change, skill building, self-determination, self-help, peer support, and community integration as the foundations of mental health treatment that emphasizes hope, affirmation, participation, and productivity for consumers of mental health services in a culturally competent manner.

This organization collaborates with the National Mental Health Consumers' Self-Help Clearinghouse.

Michigan Supported Education Program

Originally a demonstration project modeled after the Boston University Center for Psychiatric Rehabilitation, this program operated in six locations in Michigan and was supported by Supported Education Community Action Group (SECAG), until it lost its funding. Nevertheless, the program continues to operate an online resource center for supported education and will speak to interested parents.

SECAG
University of Michigan School of Social Work
1080 S. University Ave. B660
Ann Arbor, MI 48109-1106
(734) 615-2119
e-mail: secag@umich.edu
www.ssw.umich.edu/sed/

National Alliance on Mental Illness (NAMI)
Colonial Place Three
2107 Wilson Blvd., Suite 300
Arlington, VA 22201-3042
(703) 524-7600
Information Helpline: (800) 950-6264 (NAMI)
www.nami.org

> NAMI is a large national organization dedicated to helping parents help their
> children with mental illness get the services they need. Organized in 1979 by
> families of people with mental illness who were frustrated by the poor quality
> of the services available to them, NAMI now has chapters, called affiliates, all
> over the United States and offers a rich array of services and opportunities.
> This is the place to start when you go looking for support and education.
> NAMI sponsors parents' groups, siblings' groups, and offers the Family-to-
> Family education program, a free 12-week course in living with a person with
> mental illness, taught by family members. NAMI's website also has many help-
> ful links and lots of information about mental illness, treatment, advocacy, and
> support.

National Association of State Mental Health Directors
66 Canal Center Plaza, Suite 302
Alexandria, VA 22314
(703) 739-9333
www.nasmhpd.org

> This is a policy-oriented nonprofit organization intended to benefit the nation's
> mental health systems. Its website provides a link to each state's office of men-
> tal health. Go to www.nasmhpd.org/mental_health_resources.cfm where you
> can click on your state and be directed to the state mental health office website.
> This same page will also link you to many relevant federal agencies.

National Dissemination Center for Children with Disabilities
P.O. Box 1492
Washington, DC 20013
(800) 695-0285
www.nichcy.org

> The Dissemination Center is sponsored by the federal government and is
> intended to help children with disabilities access services to which they are

entitled. Funded by the Office of Special Education Programs (OSEP) at the U.S. Department of Education, the Center website maintains many links to resources parents may find useful for children and adolescents who are considered psychiatrically disabled.

National Empowerment Center (NEC), Inc.
599 Canal Street
Lawrence, MA 01841
(800) POWER2U or (800) 769-3728
www.power2u.org

NEC is a "consumer/survivor/expatient-run organization and each of us is living a personal journey of recovery and empowerment. We are convinced that recovery and empowerment are not the privilege of a few exceptional leaders, but rather are possible for each person who has been diagnosed with mental illness." NEC operates a toll-free information and referral line, Monday through Friday, EST, during regular work hours, in English and Spanish, covering a broad range of topics such as legal information and the location of self-help groups. They also keep lists of advocacy groups run by consumers in all 50 states.

National Institute of Mental Health
Office of Communications
6001 Executive Boulevard, Room 8184, MSC 9663
Bethesda, MD 20892-9663
(866) 615-6464
www.nimh.nih.gov

National Mental Health Association (NMHA)
2001 N. Beauregard Street, 12th Floor
Alexandria, VA 22311
(800) 969-6642
www.nmha.org

Founded in 1909 by ex-mental patient Clifford Beers, NMHA is the oldest mental health organization in the United States and its 340+ affiliates are dedicated to promoting mental health, prevention, advocacy, education, and research. Unlike NAMI, their focus is not specifically on parents, but they have hotlines and other helpful services available.

National Mental Health Consumers' Self-Help Clearinghouse
1211 Chestnut Street, Suite 1207
Philadelphia, PA 19107
(800) 553-4539 or (215) 751-1810
e-mail: info@mhselfhelp.org
www.mhselfhelp.org/program.html

Founded in 1986, this group was established and is run by ex-mental patients (consumers), and they have all kinds of resources and services to offer people who want to start self-help groups. Their goal is to "reject the label of 'those who cannot help themselves.'"

National Mental Health Information Center
Substance Abuse and Mental Health Services Administration
P.O. Box 42557
Washington, DC 20015
Information hotline: (800) 789-2647 (8:30-5:00 EST)
www.mentalhealth.org

The information center, sponsored by the federal government, was developed for users of mental health services and their families, the general public, policymakers, providers, and the media. Information Center staff members are available to answer questions, directing callers to federal, state, and local organizations involved in the treatment and prevention of mental illness.

National Schizophrenia Foundation
403 Seymour Street
Suite 202
Lansing, MI 48933
(517) 485-7168
Consumer Line: (800) 482-9534
e-mail: info@nsfoundation.org
www.NSFoundation.org

The National Schizophrenia Foundation (NSF) is a not-for-profit organization that promotes public awareness, educates the public about schizophrenia, and administers the Schizophrenics Anonymous (SA) self-help network. The first SA support group was founded in Detroit in 1985 by a woman with schizophrenia who sought to create a support group for herself and others diagnosed with the illness and related disorders. Now there are 175 SA support groups across the United States and abroad. You can find out if there is a group near you by calling the consumer 800 number listed above.

Recovery, Inc.
802 North Dearborn Street
Chicago, IL 60610
(312) 337-5661
e-mail: inquiries@recovery-inc.org
www.recovery-inc.com/meetings.htm

Active since 1937, Recovery, Inc., sponsors over 700 self-help groups for people with all mental and emotional disorders. Their website makes it easy to find a group in your area.

Schizophrenics Anonymous
(See description under the listing for National Schizophrenia Foundation.)

United States Psychiatric Rehabilitation Association
601 North Hammonds Ferry Rd, Suite A
Linthicum, MD 21090
(410) 789-7054 or (410) 789-7682 TDD
e-mail: info@uspra.org
www.uspra.org

> Formerly known as IAPSRS, this organization is concerned with the delivery
> of rehabilitation services—social and vocational—to psychiatric patients. It
> may be a useful organization to join for parents interested in political activism.

The Village Integrated Service Agency
456 Elm Avenue
Long Beach, CA 90802
(562) 437-6717
e-mail: village1@pacbell.net
www.village-isa.org

> The mission statement of the Village Integrated Service Agency is as follows:
> - To support and teach adults with psychiatric disabilities to recognize their
>   strengths and power to successfully live, socialize, and work in the community
> - To stimulate and promote system-wide changes necessary so that these in-
>   dividuals may achieve these goals.

Vinfen Corporation
950 Cambridge Street
Cambridge, MA 02141
(617) 441-7170
www.vinfen.org

> According to their website, "Vinfen is a private, non-profit human services
> organization providing a comprehensive array of services to adults and chil-
> dren with mental illness, mental retardation, and behavioral health disabilities.
> Our mission statement underscores that we are in the business of 'transform-
> ing lives.'"

WestBridge Community Services
90 Sherman Street
Cambridge, MA 02140
(800) 889-7871
e-mail: info@westbridge.org

> WestBridge is a private agency brought into existence by the family of a person
> diagnosed with both schizophrenia and substance use disorder. It is "dedicated to
> supporting the recovery of families and individuals who experience co-occurring
> mental illness and substance use disorders. . . . At WestBridge, that means mov-
> ing beyond the boundaries of a traditional treatment facility, developing instead
> an understanding for the needs and strengths of individuals and their families."
> Their emphasis on the family as well as the individual is unusual.

Windhorse Community Services, Inc.
1501 Yarmouth Ave.
Boulder, CO 80304
(303) 786-9314 (ext. 101)
info@windhorsecommunityservices.com

Windhorse Associates, Inc.
211 North Street, Suite #1
Northampton, MA 01060
(413) 586-0207 (ext. 113)
(877) 844-8181 (ext. 113)
www.windhorseassociates.org

Located in Boulder, Colorado, and Northampton, Massachusetts, Windhorse is a "therapeutic community approach to recovery" dedicated to providing a form of alternative treatment to a diverse range of patients who are "struggling with extreme psychiatric disturbances." Their goal is to provide treatment to people outside of a hospital or group setting. Windhorse is a coalition of mental health professionals, consumers, and family members that believes it to be very important that these three groups work together in a way that informs the whole: "The services at Windhorse Associates are individually tailored in close communication with each client and family, and represent a wide range of intensity and structure. For a person needing intensive support, we offer a full clinical team that works with clients in home environments in the community." The strong emphasis this program places on family involvement can be appreciated by looking at the Guide for Families page of their website.

The Boulder, Colorado, program provides similar services: "WCS has worked with clients with a wide range of diagnoses and conditions, including schizophrenia and other psychotic disorders, affective disorders, substance abuse, eating disorders, personality disorders, closed-head injuries, obsessive-compulsive disorders, pervasive developmental disorders, autism, challenges of aging, and terminal illnesses."

Appendix 1

Diagnostic Criteria for Schizophrenia

A. *Characteristic symptoms*: Two (or more) of the following, each present for a significant portion of time during a 1-month period (or less if successfully treated):

(1) delusions
(2) hallucinations
(3) disorganized speech (e.g., frequent derailment or incoherence)
(4) grossly disorganized or catatonic behavior
(5) negative symptoms, i.e., affective flattening, alogia, or avolition

Note: Only one Criterion A symptom is required if delusions are bizarre or hallucinations consist of a voice keeping up a running commentary on the person's behavior or thoughts, or two or more voices conversing with each other.

B. *Social/occupational dysfunction*: For a significant portion of the time since the onset of the disturbance, one or more major areas of functioning such as work, interpersonal relations, or self-care are markedly below the level achieved prior to the onset (or when the onset is in childhood or adolescence, failure to achieve expected level of interpersonal, academic, or occupational achievement).

C. *Duration*: Continuous signs of the disturbance persist for at least 6 months. This 6-month period must include at least 1 month of symptoms (or less if successfully treated) that meet Criterion A (i.e., active-phase symptoms) and may include periods of prodromal or residual symptoms. During these pro-dromal or residual periods, the signs of the disturbance may be manifested by only negative symptoms or two or more symptoms listed in Criterion A present in an attenuated form (e.g., odd beliefs, unusual perceptual experiences).

D. *Schizoaffective and Mood Disorder exclusion:* Schizoaffective Disorder and Mood Disorder With Psychotic Features have been ruled out because either (1) no Major Depressive, Manic, or Mixed Episodes have occurred concurrently with the active-phase symptoms; or (2) if mood episodes have occurred during active-phase symptoms, their total duration has been brief relative to the duration of the active and residual periods.

E. *Substance/general medical condition exclusion:* The disturbance is not due to the direct physiological effects of a substance (e.g., drug abuse, a medication) or a general medical condition.

F. *Relationship to a Pervasive Developmental Disorder:* If there is a history of Autistic Disorder or another Pervasive Developmental Disorder, the additional diagnosis of Schizophrenia is made only if prominent delusions or hallucinations are also present for at least a month (or less if successfully treated).

Classification of longitudinal course (can be applied only after at least 1 year has elapsed since the initial onset of active-phase symptoms):

Episodic With Interepisode Residual Symptoms (episodes are defined by the reemergence of prominent psychotic symptoms); *also specify if:* **With Prominent Negative Symptoms**

Episodic With No Interepisode Residual Symptoms

Continuous (prominent psychotic symptoms are present throughout the period of observation); *also specify if:* **With Prominent Negative Symptoms**

Single Episode in Partial Remission; *also specify if:* **With Prominent Negative Symptoms**

Single Episode in Full Remission

Other or Unspecified Pattern

Source: Reprinted by permission from the *Diagnostic and Statistical Manual of Mental Disorders.* Copyright 2000. American Psychiatric Association.

Appendix 2

Assertive Community Treatment (ACT) and Supported Employment Programs

In 2003, the National Association of State Mental Health Program Directors Research Institute surveyed all 50 of the states plus the District of Columbia to see whether they had implemented various evidence-based services for the seriously mentally ill. Some states did not respond to the survey, for unknown reasons. The results concerning ACT programs and Supported Employment are shown in the tables on the following pages, by state. Use the NASMHPD website to find your state mental health office for further information about these programs and their availability in your state: www.nasmhpd.org/mental_health_resources.cfm

Assertive Community Treatment (ACT) and Supported Employment Programs: Breakdown by State

State	ACT programs	Supported employment
Alabama	In some localities	In some localities
Alaska	No	In some localities
Arizona	In some localities	Statewide
Arkansas	In some localities	In some localities
California	In some localities	Statewide
Colorado	In some localities	In some localities
Connecticut	In some localities	Statewide
Delaware	Statewide	Statewide
D.C.	Statewide	In some localities
Florida	Statewide	In some localities
Georgia	In some localities	Statewide
Hawaii	In some localities	In some localities
Idaho	In some localities	Statewide
Illinois	Statewide	Statewide
Indiana	In some localities	Planning to implement
Iowa	Did not respond to survey	Did not respond to survey
Kansas	In some localities	Statewide
Kentucky	In some localities	In some localities
Louisiana	In some localities	In some localities
Maine	Statewide	Statewide
Maryland	Pilot program	In some localities
Massachusetts	Statewide	Statewide
Michigan	Did not respond to survey	Did not respond to survey
Minnesota	In some localities	In some localities
Mississippi	Did not respond to survey	Did not respond to survey
Missouri	Pilot program	Statewide
Montana	In some localities	In some localities

Assertive Community Treatment (ACT) and Supported Employment Programs: Breakdown by State

State	ACT programs	Supported employment
Nebraska	In some localities	In some localities
Nevada	Statewide	Statewide
New Hampshire	In some localities	In some localities
New Jersey	Statewide	Statewide
New Mexico	Planning to implement	Statewide
New York	Statewide	Statewide
North Carolina	In some localities	No
North Dakota	Statewide	Statewide
Ohio	Planning to implement	Statewide
Oklahoma	In some localities	In some localities
Oregon	In some localities	In some localities
Pennsylvania	In some localities	In some localities
Rhode Island	Statewide	Statewide
South Carolina	In some localities	In some localities
South Dakota	In some localities	No
Tennessee	In some localities	In some localities
Texas	Statewide	Statewide
Utah	Pilot program	Statewide
Vermont	In some localities	Statewide
Virginia	In some localities	No
Washington	In some localities	In some localities
West Virginia	Planning to implement	Statewide
Wisconsin	Did not respond to survey	Did not respond to survey
Wyoming	Pilot program	Planning to implement

Source: National Association of State Mental Health Program Directors Research Institute (NRI), March 2004. www.nri-inc.org/Profiles02/11EBP2003.pdf. Accessed 11/23/04.

Bibliography

Allness, Deborah. "Client-centered comprehensive assessment and individual treatment planning in Assertive Community Treatment." Unpaginated, no date. Report prepared by NAMI, the National Association of State Mental Health Directors (NASMHD), and Substance Abuse and Mental Health Services Administration (SAMHSA), U.S. Department of Health and Human Services. www.nasmhpd.org/general_files/publications/tta_pubs/NAMI/PACT Guide.doc. Accessed 11/16/04.

American Academy of Child and Adolescent Psychiatry. "Schizophrenia in children." www.aacap.org/publications/factsfam/schizo.htm. Accessed 8/30/04.

American Psychiatric Association. *Diagnostic and Statistical Manual of Mental Disorders* (4th ed.). Washington, DC: American Psychiatric Association, 1994.

Arieti, Silvano. *The Interpretation of Schizophrenia* (2d ed.). New York: Basic Books, 1974.

Bateson Gregory, Don D. Jackson, Jay Haley, and John Weakland. Toward a theory of schizophrenia. *Behavioral Science* 1 (1956): 251-264.

———— A note on the double bind family process. *Family Process* 2 (1963): 154-161.

Bezchlibnyk-Butler, K. Z., and J. J. Jeffries (eds.). *Clinical Handbook of Psychotropic Drugs* (12th ed.). Seattle, WA: Hogrefe and Huber.

Bender, Eve. Variety of factors keeping people from MH care. *Psychiatric News* 39:6 (November 19, 2004). http://pn.psychiatryonline.org/cgi/content/full/39/22/6. Accessed 11/30/04.

Bottoms, Greg. *Angelhead: My Brother's Descent into Madness*. New York: Crown Publishers, 2000.

Bustillo, J. R., J. Lauriello, and S. J. Keith. Schizophrenia: Improving outcome. *Harvard Review of Psychiatry* 6 (1999): 229-240.

Chovil, Ian. "The experience of schizophrenia." www.chovil.com. Accessed 11/8/04.

Deveson, Anne. *Tell Me I'm Here: One Family's Experience of Schizophrenia*. New York: Penguin Books, 1991.

Drugs vs. talk therapy: 3,079 readers rate their care for depression and anxiety. *Consumer Reports* 69 (October 2004): 22-29.

Evans, Dwight L., Edna B. Foa, Raquel E. Gur, Herbert Hendin, Charles P. O'Brien, Martin E. P. Seligman, and B. Timothy Walsh. *Treating and Preventing Adolescent Mental Health Disorders: What We Know and What We Don't Know—A Research Agenda for Improving the Mental Health of Our Youth*. New York: Oxford University Press with the Annenberg Foundation Trust at Sunnylands and the Annenberg Public Policy Center at the University of Pennsylvania, 2005.

Frith, Christopher, and Eve Johnstone. *Schizophrenia: A Very Short Introduction*. Oxford, UK: Oxford University Press, 2003.

Fromm-Reichmann, Frieda. Notes on the development of treatment of schizophrenia by psychoanalytic psychotherapy. In *Psychoanalysis and Psychotherapy: Selected Papers*. Chicago: University of Chicago Press, 1959.

Gilman, Charlotte Perkins. *The Yellow Wallpaper*. New York: The Feminist Press, 1973.

"Green, Hannah" (Greenberg, Joanne). *I Never Promised You a Rose Garden*. New York: Signet/New American Library, 1964.

Johnson, Ann Braden. *Out of Bedlam: The Truth About Deinstitutionalization*. New York: Basic Books, 1990.

"Jump Start Initiative." Recovery & Rehabilitation 2003; vol. 2, no. 4. www.bu.edu/cpr/rr/jumpstart/rr-jumpstart.html. Accessed 11/23/04.

Kaplan, Harold I., and Benjamin J. Sadock. *Synopsis of Psychiatry* (8th ed.). Baltimore: Lippincott Williams and Wilkins, 1998.

Keltner, N. L., and D. G. Folks. *Psychotropic Drugs* (2d ed.). St. Louis, MO: Mosby, 1997.

Leff, Julian. *The Unbalanced Mind*. New York: Columbia University Press, 2001.

Lehman, A. F., et al. Evidence-based treatment for schizophrenia. *Psychiatric Clinics of North America* 26 (2003): 939-954. [abstract]

Mental Health: A Report of the Surgeon General. www.surgeongeneral.gov/library/mentalhealth/home.html. Accessed 11/19/04.

Moorman, Margaret. *My Sister's Keeper: Learning to Cope with a Sibling's Mental Illness*. New York: Penguin Books, 1992.

Moran, Mark. Schizophrenia treatment should focus on recovery, not just symptoms. *Psychiatric News* 39 (November 19, 2004): 24. http://pn.psychiatryonline.org/cgi/content/full/39/22/04. Accessed 11/30/04.

Mowbray, Carol. Rehab rounds: The Michigan supported education program. *Psychiatric Services* 51 (2000): 1355-1357. http://ps.psychiatryonline.org/cgi/content/full/51/11/1355. Accessed 12/2/04.

Nasar, Sylvia. *A Beautiful Mind*. New York: Simon and Schuster, 1998.

National Alliance on Mental Illness. "Early onset schizophrenia; Medicaid basics; about NAMI." www.nami.org. Accessed 8/30/04.

National Institute of Mental Health. "Schizophrenia." www.nimh.nih.gov/publicat/schizoph/cfm. Accessed 8/30/04.

Neugeboren, Jay. *Imagining Robert: My Brother, Madness, and Survival.* New York: William Morrow and Company, 1997.

——. *Transforming Madness: New Lives for People Living with Mental Illness.* New York: William Morrow and Company, 1999.

Physicians' Desk Reference (58th ed.). Montvale, NJ: Thomson PDR, 2004.

Shapiro, Sue A. *Contemporary Theories of Schizophrenia: Review and Synthesis.* New York: McGraw-Hill, 1981.

Simon, Clea. *Mad House: Growing Up in the Shadow of Mentally Ill Siblings.* New York: Doubleday, 1997.

Swados, Elizabeth. *The Four of Us: A Family Memoir.* New York: Farrar, Straus and Giroux, 1991.

Temes, Roberta. *Getting Your Life Back Together When You Have Schizophrenia.* Oakland, CA: New Harbinger Publications, 2002.

Torrey, E. Fuller. *Surviving Schizophrenia: A Manual for Families, Consumers, and Providers* (4th ed.). New York: Quill, 2001.

Tsuang Ming T., and Stephen V. Faraone. *Schizophrenia: The Facts* (2d ed.). Oxford, UK: Oxford University Press, 1997.

Vonnegut, Mark. *The Eden Express.* New York: Bantam Books, 1976.

Wechsler, James A. *In a Darkness.* New York: Irvington Publishers, 1983.

Woolis, Rebecca. *When Someone You Love Has a Mental Illness: A Handbook for Family, Friends, and Caregivers.* New York: Jeremy Tarcher/Perigee, 1992.

Wyden, Peter. *Conquering Schizophrenia: A Father, His Son, and a Medical Breakthrough.* New York: Alfred A. Knopf, 1998.

Index

About the Authors

Raquel E. Gur, M.D., Ph.D., is Professor of Psychiatry, Neurology and Radiology at the University of Pennsylvania in Philadelphia, where she has acted as Director of the Neuropsychiatry Section and the Schizophrenia Research Center. Her academic career has been devoted to the study of brain function in schizophrenia.

Ann Braden Johnson, Ph.D., is a medical writer whose work has included both highly technical articles in medical journals and educational materials for patients. A psychotherapist by training, she spent twenty-five years designing and administering mental health programs. She is the author of *Out of Bedlam: The Truth about De-institutionalization.*